SERVICE · INCLUDED

SERVICE · INCLUDED

Four-Star
Secrets
of an
Eavesdropping
Waiter

•

Phoebe Damrosch

WILLIAM MORROW

An Imprint of HarperCollins*Publishers*

Grateful acknowledgment is made to reprint excerpts from *The French Laundry Cookbook*, copyright © 1999 by Thomas Keller. Used by permission of Artisan, a division of Workman Publishing Co., Inc., New York. All rights reserved.

HarperCollins books may be purchased for educational, business, or sales promotional use. For information please write: Special Markets Department, HarperCollins Publishers, 10 East 53rd Street, New York, NY 10022.

FIRST EDITION

Designed by Nicola Ferguson

Library of Congress Cataloging-in-Publication Data

Damrosch, Phoebe, 1978–
   Service included: four-star secrets of an eavesdropping waiter / Phoebe Damrosch.
     p. cm.
   ISBN: 978-0-06-122814-8
   ISBN-10: 0-06-122814-1
   1. Damrosch, Phoebe, 1978– 2. Waitresses—United States—Biography. 3. Per Se (Restaurant) 4. Food Service—New York (State)—New York—Anecdotes. I. Title.

TX910.5.D36A3 2007
647.95092—dc22
  [B]   2007061198

07 08 09 10 11 ID/RRD 10 9 8 7 6

1/08 Pur

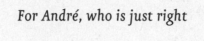

For André, who is just right

• contents •

• a diner's bill of rights •

---

1. The right to have your reservation honored

2. The right to water

3. The right to the food you ordered at
   the temperature the chef intended

4. The right to a clean, working bathroom

5. The right to clean flatware, glassware,
   china, linen, tables, and napkins

6. The right to enough light to read your menu

7. The right to hear your dining companions
   when they speak

8. The right to be served until the restaurant's
   advertised closing time

9. The right to stay at your table as long as you like

10. The right to salt and pepper

• introduction •

I USUALLY SKIP introductions and plunge right into the first chapter. At the end, if I loved the book, I savor everything to delay its inevitable close—even the history of the font. I imagine that reading an introduction at the beginning is like dunking a toe in to check the literary temperature. Your toe, in this case, will experience: an ambiguous disclaimer about fact and fiction, a feeble attempt to summarize this book, an explanation of the title, and a statement of prophylactic contrition.

As to the slippery subject of nonfiction, all I can say is that this book contains the truth according to my memory, with the following exceptions: consolidation of conversations, time, and two characters. I altered a few names and incriminating details and left a great deal out, mainly that which would have embarrassed, angered, or hurt people unnecessarily.

While I worked on this project, well-meaning friends and acquaintances asked what I was writing about, a question for which I was always ill-prepared. At first I told outrageous lies (see "City Love"). After lying backfired, I tried to be vague: "It's about restaurant culture. . . ." When pressed, I gave a laundry list of topics: food, fine dining, love, jealousy, New York, late-night grazing, guests, cookbooks, critics. Eyes glazed over. The next approach was reverse psychology. This book is not a sepia-toned portrait of my grandmother in the kitchen making meatballs, samosas, congee, or empanadas. It is not a how-to; you will find nary a recipe, nor will you learn to bone, butterfly, boil, or braise. It is not a history of great breadth; most of the story occurs within an eighteen-month period.

After I left Per Se restaurant, the setting of this book, a former colleague passed along a story that the chef told the staff. If you want to understand commitment, he explained, all you have to do is look at the American breakfast of bacon and eggs. The chicken was involved, but the pig was committed.

This is a story about commitment: to food, service, love, perfection, and to being the bacon.

Rated PG: May contain material offensive to Republicans, vegans, pharmaceutical lobbyists, and those on a low-sodium diet. Animals were harmed during the writing of this book.

• the art of the day job •

EVENTUALLY I HAD to accept that I wasn't working in restaurants to support my art like most of my coworkers; I was posing as an artist to justify my work as a waiter. The small café where I worked in Williamsburg, Brooklyn, employed artists as if there were quotas to be met: a drummer, a filmmaker, an actor, a dancer, a photographer, a designer, and myself—who at that point fancied herself a writer. Every so often someone would go on tour, decide to move back to some small town in some small state, or simply leave out of frustration with what he or she wasn't getting to do. It's a dangerous combination, this dichotomy of artist/waiter, one that often leads to listless service and half-finished Margaritas forgotten behind the computer.

I lived in a studio apartment upstairs from my high school sweetheart in Williamsburg (recently rated the hippest neighborhood in America—how scientific a study that was, I hardly know). We had broken up three years before and were now pretending to be friends, sharing a computer and sweaters, buying groceries, building bookshelves, and sabotaging each other's love life. That we spent most of our time together in the kitchen was no surprise; food had always been our bond. Between our early experimentations and our reunion years later, we had grown confident in our techniques and ambitious in our undertakings, mastering emulsifications and reductions, the art of kneading, and the importance of letting things rest. He played the chef, and I the visionary, reading recipes out loud from the floor, my back against the refrigerator door.

When I found myself without a job, my ex-love suggested that I interview at the café where he worked. I would shoot for a busboy position since I had no experience in the business. When the manager asked if I knew how to make a cappuccino, I said in all seriousness that I didn't, but that I drank a lot of them. I have no idea why she hired me.

The café modeled itself after a funny amalgamation of cultures, from its curved mosaic ceiling to the eclectic cuisine, which I called Middleterranean: scrambled eggs with coriander and ginger, lamb shank with currants and pine nuts, salmon on Israeli couscous. Having just escaped my last job on Fifth Avenue with my sanity intact (I'll get to that), I pierced my nose, dyed my new pixie cut a dramatic platinum blond, and took to keeping my corkscrew, or wine key, tucked into knee-high boots. The café was perhaps best known for brunch, when the line ran out the door and we mastered the art of sprinting while balancing three or four coffee cups. Bed-headed hipsters make challenging brunch guests, barely able to utter their Bloody Mary order, let alone abide a wait for their eggs Barbarosa with crawfish and chorizo. Margaritas were essential to survival.

I was the only busboy not named Mohammed. Here, as in many restaurants around the city, any deviation from the distinct class/race hierarchy makes everyone uneasy. In most New York restaurants, the chef is Caucasian, the waiters are starving artists, the busboys are from Bangladesh, and the kitchen workers and dishwashers are from Latin America. I honestly think I was promoted so quickly from busboy to waiter because the chef and the waiters felt uncomfortable asking me to mop up their spills, take out the trash, and clean the windows. I certainly wasn't promoted for my skill or knowledge. When I came to the kitchen to pick up a salad, the cooks took a moment longer to anchor the teetering greens between beet support beams. They knew that when I picked up a bowl of soup the crostini, which was supposed to remain on the rim of the bowl, would be launched like a life raft into turbulent waves of soup. The foam on my soy chai resembled dish suds. I thought Cristal was a china company.

And yet, what better way to begin my career in the business than with a restaurant rife with clichés: roaches in the dry goods, mice everywhere, shady finances, messy love affairs, drugs, theft, basement flooding, and chefs with a penchant for throwing pots, pans, and produce. I lasted more than a year, in which time I saw at least ten waiters and two chefs come and go. We were always out of more than half the wines on the wine list and often couldn't locate the other half. The reservation system was a pile of Post-its.

When the neighborhood really started to boom and became saturated with new restaurants even hipper than ours, business lagged. The owners, whose only restaurant experience had been to piece this one together with duct tape and borrowed money, responded by hiring a real manager. They couldn't afford a seasoned one, so they found a cheap one. Enter Jessica, a smoky twenty-four-year-old with a severe bob and a crafty, brooding look. She fit right into the scene, with her leg warmers and short skirts, her carefully smudged eyeliner, and a tube of red lipstick she used as a bookmark in the new reservation book. Within months, both her drug habit and the fact that she was sleeping with the chef were common knowledge. One day she simply disappeared, leaving behind one black sneaker and a mirror. For a while, I took over many of her responsibilities: ordering wine, scheduling the Mohammeds, and planning private parties. The more involved I became in the business, the shadier I realized it was. We owed money to everyone and paid them off only when we needed to order something else.

I only began working in restaurants after I had exhausted quite a few other nontraditional ways of making a living. I had written a Web page for a Filipino dating service. I had walked a dog. I had consolidated online food reviews (my first and last desk job, lasting a whole six weeks). I had proofread for law firms, babysat for JFK's three grandchildren, and helped organize documentary film viewings at women's prisons. For two years after college, I pretended that I was about to apply to Ph.D. English literature programs, mostly because I had been in school my whole life and couldn't imagine anything else.

After all that, I somehow got a job as a role model/nanny/errand girl for a wealthy family on Fifth Avenue. Since the household staff included two other nannies, a housekeeper, a chauffeur, a yoga instructor, a masseuse, a hair stylist, a self-tan applier, instructors of piano, Hebrew, math, and etiquette for the children, a storage expert, and a personal assistant, there was really very little for me to do. My favorite days were those when their personal chef arrived, flanked by two doormen bearing Fairway bags. Although mostly she made organic chicken nuggets from scratch for the children, she also created multicourse extravaganzas for the mother and father, who were, respectively, anorexic and overworked, and left the poached salmon and tarte tatins to the nannies. I took the job because the afternoon hours allowed me to pretend to be a writer, but after a summer of commuting from the Upper East Side to the Hamptons on a bus full of housekeepers, cooks, and other nannies, it occurred to me that I might work similar hours in a different setting. At the beach there were eight bedrooms straight out of *Coastal Living*, ocean views, and an incredibly well-stocked Sub-Zero (the personal chef also commuted), and yet, I felt like I was on house arrest.

I suppose I could have found a job in publishing like a good English major, but as far as I was concerned, offices were dusty, stagnant, and badly lit. Kitchens, on the other hand, had a pulse. And unlike nannying, where I took a dysfunctional role in a dysfunctional family not even my own, clearing tables and pouring water seemed to demand a very simple, tangible skill set. Plus, I could work in Brooklyn, get to know my neighbors, and cut the commute down to seconds. The other side of this, of course, was the possibility of becoming a middle-aged diner waitress with varicose veins and a smoker's cough. I vowed never to utter the phrase "Hot your coffee?" or address anyone as "hon." At family gatherings, I could hear the questions behind the questions. So what was I doing these days? (What was I doing with my terrifyingly expensive college education?) What were my plans? (When would I get a real job?) I told everyone I was writing and waiting to hear from graduate schools, but I had not written a word on anything but a cashier's check in months. I had, indeed, applied to graduate school, but not to study anything practical. I had chosen creative nonfiction—a genre as staunch in its ambivalence as I was in studying it. Furthermore, applying to the schools I had selected was not a career move, per se; all three deemphasized grading, deadlines, and job placement.

Much more pressing was my acute heartbreak. The high school sweetheart/actor/waiter downstairs, with whom I worked at the restaurant when he wasn't in rehearsal, had the audacity to fall in love with someone other than myself. The bastard. So there I was, pining after him at work, plastering my ear to the linoleum kitchen floor to no avail, chain-smoking American Spirits on the fire escape (because that's what one does in Williamsburg), and writing bad poetry. So what if we had nothing in common besides food and a hometown? So what if he hated the city I loved, and I the country for which he longed? We could spend summers in Vermont—maybe open a little artist colony/bed-and-breakfast. When he announced that she was moving in for a while, I told myself to be rational. And then I quit my café job, gathered my savings, and bought a plane ticket to Paris. If I was going to be miserable, I might as well do it somewhere tragically, distractingly (if not conventionally) romantic.

In France, I enrolled in a language school, because I thought I should have some reason to be there besides self-pity—and because it was an easy way to find housing. As it turned out, I was placed in the home of a bitter Catholic divorcée who resented my existence. Upon my arrival at her flat in the posh district of Neuilly, she instructed me not to use the phone or the kitchen and to wear shoes at all times. Bare feet left impressions that were odious to her on her constantly waxed floors. Needless to say, I spent as little time there as possible, choosing instead to wander the streets contemplating my dismal future (alone in a dark apartment in Queens with cats and a wardrobe of green polyester suits). Croissants helped to lift my spirits, as did cheese stores with more cheeses than days in the year, café crèmes and cigarettes at outdoor cafés, wine shops with basement *caves*, and tiny restaurants with self-serve chocolate mousse in mammoth ceramic bowls. With food as my constant companion, life began to look up.

When I reached the end of my month in Paris, Madame made it clear that she did not wish to extend my stay. I had bought a return ticket for two weeks after my program ended with the vague hope of falling in love and delaying my departure. But as I found love only in a glass and on a plate, and none in the arms of the envisioned Frenchman, I decided to continue my studies elsewhere. Food studies, that is. I began in the Savoie region, famed for its hiking and alpine cheeses. I do not hike, although I do hitchhike and did so in order to get to a tiny monastery famed for its Reblochon-style cheese. I discovered a woman who made sausages from donkey meat, and I lived on baguettes and sausage for my remaining time there.

When I returned to America at the end of July, I went to spend a week with a friend, a cook who had relocated to Napa Valley in order to stalk Thomas Keller. Thomas Keller was the chef of the French Laundry, a restaurant many considered to be one of the best in the country, if not the world. My friend, whose knife skills far outshone his ability to make necessary arrangements, found himself at the end of a waiting list of young cooks who were willing to work for free in the famous kitchen. I had also been curious about the French Laundry, having drooled over the cookbook in bookstores, but was not surprised to find that we were also at the bottom of the waiting list for a reservation. Every day for a week, we put on our one nice outfit and sat in the French Laundry garden, hoping for a cancellation. Every day we were nicely turned away and forced to seek solace in local vineyards.

I arrived back in New York just in time for the stifling August heat and immediately hit the streets looking for work. I had two criteria: fast cash and good food. Having worked in only one restaurant, my plan was to start talking before they even had a chance to look down at my résumé. I got myself a job at a busy Belgian restaurant in the meatpacking district where everything but the mussels looked like something you'd be served on the red-eye to L.A. Three weeks into it, I received a call from the chef I had worked for in Brooklyn. He had quit, having never quite recovered from hurricane Jessica, as I liked to call his affair with the drugged, disappearing, sometime manager. He was opening a chichi new place in Midtown and asked me to come in and be interviewed for a job. I used the same technique in this interview, talking as much about food and the business as possible in order to keep them from looking down at my résumé. Either it worked or he pulled some strings, but I was hired.

I hadn't anticipated being so lost. Within minutes of walking in the door for my first shift, I was asking my coworkers for help. The uniform was a white shirt, black pants, brown apron, and a tie that I had to have one of the male waiters tie for me. I loosened it but kept the knot after every shift so as to avoid retying. I also used a real computer system for the first time and worked with runners, coffee servers, and maître d's. There wasn't much training for the job and most of what I learned about service came from watching the more experienced waiters around me. I carefully observed how they carried their trays, where they set the glasses, from which side they handed a guest the menu.

For about a month, I was sure I would be fired at any moment. The first time I waited on one of the owners, a dessertspoon slipped from my clammy, trembling fingers. It was about a two-foot drop, and when the spoon hit the thick white tablecloth, it bounced and rolled over to his wineglass, which, mercifully, remained upright, but rang throughout the dining room as if heralding a toast. He looked up at me with something akin to wonder from the half-moon booth, which he shared with a bigwig from the Four Seasons whom he had been trying to impress. Well, she sure didn't last long, I assumed he was thinking. But I wasn't fired; in fact, I think the look of wonder had more to do with realizing that I existed at all, that dessertspoons didn't just materialize on one's table, they were carried by an actual human—one of the sea of humans in brown aprons whose names he never considered learning when he could just call us "darlin'" or "sweetie" or "buddy."

When I relaxed into the job, I realized that a capacity to remember an order and stay calm when triple-seated (three tables arriving at once) elevated me to a status far above the worst server. Once I got over my jitters, interacting with guests was easy. People are people, even if richer than God. I began to have regulars, as I had by the end of my time in Brooklyn—only instead of cardamom French toast and black coffee, they ordered the cardamom-dusted lobster tails and premier cru Meursault. Over the course of the restaurant's opening, many well-known food writers came in: Hal Rubenstein, from *New York* magazine; Amanda Hesser and William Grimes, from the *New York Times*. *Gourmet* did a big article; the Food Network shot a show. I began seeing a few possibilities for myself in this world, but I had some catching up to do.

The one thing this place had in common with the Brooklyn café was the preponderance of artists on the staff. For this reason, when the maître d' announced one sleepy Sunday night, after I had been there for about three months, that the cast of *Queer Eye for the Straight Guy* would be sitting in my section while Chef Thomas Keller sat across the room, trading was easy. It was a simple choice for me; I didn't own a television and had never seen the show, but I had watched Chef Keller from the garden at the French Laundry. I had also heard a rumor that he might be opening a restaurant in the new Time Warner Center at Columbus Circle. If I was going to continue to work in restaurants, as was seeming likely, I wanted to work in the best. Pretty cocky words coming from someone with three restaurants' worth of experience, I told myself as soon as I had the thought. My résumé wouldn't get a toenail, let alone a restaurant-issue clog, in the door.

Requesting Chef Keller's table seemed like a perfect opportunity to introduce myself, but I soon began to doubt whether this was wise.

"Do you know what kind of persimmon the chef is using?" one of the guests called me over to ask. I later found out that this was Jonathan Benno, or J.B., who was to be the chef de cuisine at the new restaurant.

What *kind* of persimmon?

I made it through that nerve-racking audition of a shift by trying to be invisible and letting the sommelier pour everything, including the water. As soon as I got back to Brooklyn, I looked up persimmon online. Then I went straight to the human-resources page on the French Laundry Web site. I thought about the hours I had spent on that garden bench in Napa, trying to get in off the waiting list. I thought of my friend looking enviously through the windows where he could see the chefs working in a pristine kitchen. And then, for the third time in the past four months, I started tinkering with my résumé.

THE APPARENTLY NUMEROUS KINDS OF PERSIMMONS

According to California Rare Fruit Growers, persimmons grew in China before spreading to Japan and Korea. They were introduced to California in the mid-1800s, where they thrive on the moderate winters and mild summers. The fruit is full of beta-carotene, vitamin C, and potassium. Persimmons can vary in color from yellow-orange to a deep orange-red and in shape and size from that of a round tomato to that of a large acorn. Wikipedia maintains that in Korea, the dried fruit is used to make a punch called sujeonggwa and the Chinese use the dried leaves for tea. Every September, residents of Mitchell, Indiana, organize a persimmon festival, including a persimmon pudding contest. The pudding, reminiscent of pumpkin pie, is served with whipped cream. There seems to be some debate about whether persimmons are best picked after a frost, when some believe they have lost their tartness. Both camps, pre- and postfrost pickers, agree that persimmons are better the riper and softer they are.

FUYU PERSIMMON (FUYUGAKI)—J.B., who knew perfectly well that he was eating a fuyu, later explained to me that chefs like this variety because even when fully ripe, they are firmer than other persimmons, pack well, and are virtually nonastringent. It is medium-size with four subtle sides.

• food porn •

I HAD A crush on the *French Laundry Cookbook* for ages, but considered it way out of my league, both in price and in required skill. I stalked it in bookstores, ogling the glossy photographs in dark aisles and secluded corners where the only witnesses to my infatuation were other desperate faux-cook foodies who probably couldn't roast a chicken to save their lives and had to resort to drooling over centerfolds of gleaming striped bass, glistening gelée, and statuesque towers of perfectly peeled tomatoes. After canapés and soups, I grew impatient and stopped caressing each page. I flipped past pepper confetti, Gewürztraminer jelly, the sculptural soft-shell crab "sandwich," and the tasting of black truffles in search of the page that made me pant: the photograph of the five-spice lobster on which a piece of foie gras rested with one sweatlike bead of fat hanging, teasing, yearning to fall. Satisfied, I caught my breath, crawled out from my corner, and slipped the book back into place between its unworthy neighbors. Surely it was a $50 example of what Anthony Bourdain calls "food porn." This is not restaurant cooking for the home chef; this is a secret pleasure for the jealous voyeur.

And this voyeur was about to get more than a peep. Despite the fact that I probably uttered fewer than fifty words to Chef Keller's table when I had waited on them a few weeks before, I managed to land an interview for Per Se, as his new restaurant was to be called. In Latin, *per se* means "in and of itself." The name Per Se was meant to distinguish it from the French Laundry, its West Coast parent. I was thrilled about the interview, but had no idea how to prepare, especially after the persimmon incident. So I bought the book. The bookstore where I found a used copy for $30 wrapped it, appropriately, in a brown paper bag. I held it close on the subway home with a sort of sheepish pride. Once home, I curled up in the corner of my couch, intent to memorize every face, term, and potentially obscure detail that might impress my future bosses. This time, I didn't allow myself to get distracted by breasts and shanks, as I previously had in bookstores. This time I read every word.

There is no doubt that the *French Laundry Cookbook* is an impressive work. Chef Keller is as interested in the sources of his ingredients and the evolution of his relationship to food as he is in the actual recipes. Before delving into preparations, he tells a story to whet your reading appetite; how he was inspired to create the dish, the discovery of a certain obscure ingredient, or the story of his first time making it. There is a section devoted to his initial experimentation with hollandaise sauce and another delineating chicken bondage (technically called trussing). We meet Ingrid Bengis, an author and Russian scholar who ships live lobsters from her home in Maine; Keith Martin, the stockbroker who retired in order to raise lambs in

Pennsylvania; John Mood, a commercial pilot who still flies despite the demands of his ten thousand palm trees, from which come the hearts of palm found on page seventy.

The book also explains Chef Keller's philosophy toward cooking, namely his famous law of diminishing returns, in which he reduces the size of his many courses to make room for a variety of flavors and textures. At the French Laundry, he constructs his menu in order to give only enough to "satisfy your appetite and pique your curiosity," enough to have you beg for "just one more bite." The other side of this law is the abundance of extravagance. "I want people to know what foie gras is all about," he writes. "I go overboard with truffles and caviar too, so that people who have perhaps only eaten truffles in stingy quantities can taste them and say 'Oh, now I understand.'" This philosophy helps explain the packed reservation book, but it is hard to imagine the home cook buying all the truffles, foie gras, and caviar needed to replicate a meal from this book without going broke on one dinner party. I almost did a few weeks later, on one dish alone.

After reading all night, I went to my interview. As the restaurant was still under construction, we met in a conference room on the floor below. I was glad I had done my research. When they asked what I knew about the French Laundry, I recited a few facts about the building, how it had been a saloon and brothel before being converted into a French steam laundry. When they asked what I thought of Chef Keller's cooking, I spoke about the intellect and playfulness of his food. When they asked if I owned the cookbook, I proudly said that I did. But when a previously silent Frenchman looked across the long boardroom table and asked if I had ever tried to make anything from the book, I paused and admitted that I had not. "Don't even try the cornets," he advised. "They break."

He was speaking of salmon cornets, the first recipe in the cookbook and the first item served to any guest at the French Laundry. The dish is made to look exactly like an ice cream cone. The difference is that the three-inch cone or cornet, named for its horn shape, retains a touch of sweetness, but is definitely savory. Black sesame seeds add a texture to its buttery crunch. The cookbook shows a picture of a waiter, actually the torso and arm of a waiter, holding two tiny cones in a tray. The cornets, tucked in paper napkins, point down through dime-sized holes in the tray. A scoop of salmon tartare with flecks of chive rests on each cone, which is filled with a red onion crème fraîche.

After serving the cornet at the French Laundry for years, introducing it at Per Se became especially important to Chef Keller. The idea for the cornet had been conceived in New York. In 1990 Chef Keller reluctantly left the city after his experimental and well-reviewed restaurant, Rakel, closed in the economic downturn of the late 1980s. He had a job lined up at a hotel in L.A., at which he was supposed to debut with a food-and-wine benefit to wow his new clientele. Before he left New York, he met a few friends for a farewell dinner in Chinatown, followed by an ice cream cone at Baskin-Robbins, as was their tradition. When the man behind the counter placed the cone in a little holder, the idea came to him. He would serve ice cream cones at the dinner, with tuna tartare instead of ice cream and a savory tuile instead of the traditional cone. They were a hit in L.A. and at many dinners since (although he now uses salmon instead of tuna); the cornet has become his most famous dish.

A few days after our conversation about cornets, the smirking Frenchman and company offered me a job as a backserver at Per Se. I accepted the position without a clue as to what it would entail. I would have taken the job for the month of training alone. Besides going to culinary school or enrolling in intensive butler training, I could think of no better place to learn about food and service. The option of veering off my current path, toward academia, publishing, or journalism remained, but it was far from tempting. I had begun to take graduate writing workshops one day a week but had yet to find my subject. For now, work and school were two distinct realms. I had no idea where either would lead, so for now I planned to pay careful attention and take notes.

Close to a month after my interview, the restaurant was still under construction. Because of this, orientation took place down the street at the Hudson Hotel. It was an especially snowy January, and before entering the large conference room where our orientation would begin, I waited with a few shivering Californians to check our coats and boots. Quite a number of French Laundry staff, both kitchen and front of the house, had come to help open Per Se. Many stayed in apartments the company had rented on Fifty-seventh Street, a building with which I would become intimately familiar in the coming months.

The general manager, Laura Cunningham, and the wine director, Paul Roberts, were standing by the door and officially introduced themselves. I recognized both from the party I had waited on weeks before. She was tall and slim, with long, dark hair pulled into an elegant and immaculate ponytail. But her most striking feature was a pair of orblike blue eyes whose intense gaze had made me sweat the other night and was now fixing to do the same. She shook my hand and said a quiet hello before Paul broke in.

"It's the captain who doesn't speak!" he teased.

The room was a sea of suits, each captain, backserver, runner, and coffee server trying his best to look four-star, each cook wearing a suit and tie, probably the only time he had worn one all year. When I walked into that room, I didn't look for Chef Keller, nor did I notice that I was underdressed in my wrinkled work pants and cardigan sweater. I saw only the ratio of my painfully single female self to the gaggle of young male chefs. It was encouraging.

I took an empty seat next to a cute blond and batted my eyelashes at him as he cheerfully told me about his recent move to New York and how he planned to open his own place back home in California after a year or so. With his girlfriend. That was exactly what I deserved, and I knew it. Back to business, I faced forward and scanned the room for Chef Keller.

I remember the chef's first speech to us partly because I was taking notes like a good little overachiever and partly because it might best be titled "The Greatest Hits of Thomas Keller." I once went to a Willie Nelson concert at a state fair and couldn't believe my luck when he played the old favorites, one after the other. In fact, literally all of them appeared on my Willie Nelson *Super Hits* album: "On the Road Again," "My Heroes Have Always Been Cowboys," "Georgia," "Always on My Mind." How many times has he played these tunes, I wondered as I sang along between bites of funnel cake. When he wanted us to join in on the chorus, he curled his right hand up as if pretending to shoot and aimed it toward the sky, where it bobbed until he hit a verse and needed it back. I don't know how Thomas would feel about the comparison, but rumor has it he's a big Lyle Lovett fan. In any case, he hit all the highlights, those I had read about in the cookbook and in interviews, and it was clear that he was as passionate in that moment as he was the first time he uttered the words. He spoke of his hero, Fernand Point, a Michelin three-star chef who died in 1955 and whom many consider the father of contemporary French cuisine; told the story of learning patience by making hollandaise sauce; explained how killing a rabbit taught him to respect his ingredients; and introduced the law of diminishing returns to those who hadn't spent, like me, the previous night fondling the cookbook. The law in its simplest form: more is less.

Much ado is made about celebrity chefs and their presence in the kitchen. Clearly, it is impossible for chefs who operate many restaurants to be in their kitchens at all times. But, as I see it, this is not necessarily a deficiency. The chefs are the visionaries and leaders, but they have working under them a team of highly qualified cooks who are, hopefully, as good or better at the day-to-day aspects of running the kitchen. In a few years, these men and women will go on to be the celebrities who are chastised for not being in their kitchens.

Chef Keller planned to spend the first few months training the Per Se staff and overseeing the opening. During this time, the French Laundry would undergo renovations. After he had ensured that Per Se could run smoothly, he would head back to California and reopen the French Laundry. From then on, he would split his time between the two restaurants, while also tending to his newly opened bistro, Bouchon, in Las Vegas. This, as you will see, is not exactly what happened.

It occurred to me at the end of our first day of training that if I were a skeptic, I might find this whole thing a little cultish. There were philosophies, laws, uniforms, elaborate rituals, an unspoken code of honor and integrity, and, most important, a powerful leader. But I am not a skeptic; I drank the Kool-Aid. I sat there, eagerly taking notes in the little book I had bought for that very purpose, feeling proud to be one of the chosen. So I knew practically nothing about wine or fish knives and felt like a fake pronouncing French food terminology (despite my recent visit to France, I still preferred to point and mumble when I ordered croissants). At least I knew we were all starting at the beginning and that we all had the same goal: finesse.

Unfortunately, I could think of few people in my life who would be receptive to this particular gospel. None of my friends or family even understood why I was excited about another job waiting tables, and the only person I knew on the staff was someone I had had the bad luck of working with previously. This guy was a rare case: an actor who loved the restaurant business and was taking a break from performing to devote himself to waiting tables. Unfortunately, you can take the actor out of the performance, but you can't take the performance out of the actor, and watching this guy explain the menu as if he were Henry V on St. Crispin's Day sent me fleeing from the dining room on many an occasion. I would prefer to chew on tinfoil. So I was on my own for the evening. I could watch *Babette's Feast* again, or I could show the little voice in my head what I was made of—the little voice that kept whispering, "Don't even try the cornets. They break."

WHEN I GOT back to Brooklyn, I scanned the list of ingredients: flour, sugar, salt, butter, eggs, black sesame seeds. I checked the flour for worms. Good to go. I didn't have any black sesame seeds, but that hardly seemed compulsory. My cornets would be unashamed of their nakedness. "Cornets Before the Fall," I would call them. I also figured I could use regular table salt instead of kosher. How different could salt be?

The recipe calls for a hollow circular stencil, whatever that was. I searched my cabinets for a substitute, settling at last on an old hummus container that was a little warped, but certainly roundish. I did as I was told, awkwardly cutting the plastic of the hummus container into the semblance of a hollow ring. Since I didn't have a Silpat (the silicone surface used most often in making pastry to eliminate sticking), I spooned my cone batter onto a nonstick baking pan using the homemade hummus mold, which I had to wrestle into submission with increasingly sticky fingers. The first batch burned in half the estimated cooking time. The second batch I made thicker and cooked less, but when I tried to lift them from the pan they bunched up into a wrinkled beige mass. I knew that anyone I might call to commiserate with would want to know exactly why this had occurred as an appealing endeavor for an unskilled, ill-equipped single woman in a fourth-floor walk-up in Brooklyn on a cold winter weeknight. Not exactly a recipe for an impromptu cocktail party. At one time I would have called my ex-friend downstairs, who loved nothing more than aiding a damsel in distress, especially when it meant flexing his culinary might. In despair, I trashed the cornets, dumped the dirty dishes into the sink, and slumped down the block to D.O.C. for wine and cheese, my solution to all of life's ills. Diego, my favorite waiter in the city, greeted me as always with his big Dick Van Dyke grin and poured me a little "som-a-thing e-special" from the south of Italy. My wine knowledge needed improvement, but for the moment I drowned my sorrows indiscriminately and fantasized about breaking up with the cookbook. It's not you, it's me—I'm just not ready for a Silpat and a hollow circular mold right now.

AS I RECALL, the next few days of training were mostly administrative. The human resources director went through health insurance and dental, both practically unheard of for restaurant workers. There was the option of a 401(k), which,

I will be honest, goes under the heading of "Things That Took Me a Long Time to Embrace/Understand," well below hand-bags, heels, lipstick, and a few other things I would have to know you better to list. There were forms to be signed, maps of the building, biographies of management, and fact sheets about Chef Keller's other restaurants: the French Laundry in California, and his two bistros in California and Las Vegas, both called Bouchon. And there were rules. Many of them were of the usual no-smoking, no-gum-chewing variety, but a few caught my attention.

Rule #4: No cologne, scented lotions, scented soaps, aftershave, or perfume are to be worn during service.

Over the next year there were offenders to that rule, which was enforced by our peers even more severely than by our bosses. If I was to be parted from my Old Spice men's deodor-ant (which I love, inexplicably, almost as much as I love John-son's Baby Lotion), some doe-eyed kitchen server sure as hell wasn't about to traipse in smelling all sexy and musky. I would make sure of it.

The point of this rule, of course, was to make sure that nothing interfered with the guests' enjoyment of their food and wine. For the same reason, there was no art on the walls or music in the room: the focus was on the food and the expe-rience of dining.

A corollary to the rule, one we would discuss extensively during our training, defined how present we were to be when serving people. When I think of scents, I think of an enticing Frenchwoman in a slim skirt suit and knotted scarf and a cloud of Chanel in her wake. In contrast, the goal of a good waiter is to be present when needed or wanted, but also to disappear when not needed or wanted. That is hard to do when you smell like a bottle of Pantene Pro-V. And who knows—maybe the guest's ex-wife used Pantene. Best not to take a chance.

Rule #20: When asked, guide guests to the bathroom instead of pointing.

I understand the logic of this. I hate wandering around restaurants, opening broom closets and storage rooms looking for the ladies' room. Even when someone says it's around the corner and to my right, I still manage to end up in the coffee station. At Per Se, unless we were holding plates in our hands, we were expected to show the guest the way. I usually saw them just past the bar because at least a few times a week, guests walked into the glass wall of the wine cellar; and if they didn't walk away with a bloody nose, they certainly walked away with less dignity. After selling them the very wine that clouded their minds and blurred the line between air and glass, it hardly seemed fair to let them go unsupervised. Once past the danger zone, however, I gestured down the hallway to the well-marked bathrooms and let the guest take it from there. Even so, some of the men seemed a bit uncomfortable, as if I planned to accompany them in and help. The eighteen percent you will leave me, sir, I always wanted to say, would not cover that.

Some of my coworkers took this rule very seriously and walked guests right up to the bathroom and opened the door. If you are going to get them there, you might as well follow through, one of them explained to me. This made me very uncomfortable, but then, I am also the kind of person who gets stage fright when a bathroom attendant is present or even when peeing in someone's studio apartment.

Rule #25: Hair must be cut above the ears.

A. Women's hair must be neatly arranged off the face
B. Everyone's hair must remain as it was when they were hired. (Rule #27 explains that the same goes for facial hair.)

Of all the rules, 25(b) was the most fascinating to me. I was beginning to understand what the management meant when they spoke of "image." They didn't hire someone with pink hair or a scraggly goatee, so they wanted to make sure they didn't get stuck with one later.

I pushed the limits of this rule and got away with growing my hair out and adding streaks of various hues, but was often chided for unruliness. "Damrosch," Paolo, the Italian manager who interviewed me, would say with a nod toward a private corner, where he would look at my hair as if it were a burning bush and try to find the right words. "Your hair. It is flying away."

Rule #28: Open-toe shoes are not permitted.

The rules for men's formal shoes were straightforward and easy to follow: they had to have laces and be buffable. Not surprisingly, women's shoes proved to be more of a headache. Try finding lace-up women's shoes that aren't sneakers and don't have heels. That meant pumps and patent leather were out. Mary Janes and loafers had no laces, and boots did not count as shoes. I went to Macy's, where I tried on (and swam in) men's shoes, attempted to squeeze into boy's shoes, and eventually ended up with the AARP crowd in Comfort Shoes, trying on thick-soled numbers that also came in navy blue and beige.

Taking a cue from the kitchen, where most of the chefs wore clogs to support their backs and protect their toes, one of the runners discovered clogs with laces. They turned out to be so comfortable that, one after the other, most of us imitated her until we started referring to them as the "single white female shoes." With broad, shiny black toes and thick rubber soles, we all looked like we were riding around with Lincoln Town Cars on our feet. Come to think of it, shoes this ugly might be a form of birth control the whole country could get behind.

Rule #32: If you're going to be more than five minutes late for your shift, you must call—even if it means getting off the subway to do so.

This rule had to be written by a Californian. It's one thing if you leave your house late, but if you are stuck underground, the last thing you are going to do is get off a subway train and hope for another one. If you live on the G crosstown, which is the worst train in the city because it neither crosses town as promised nor bisects any trains to which you might want to transfer, you might not see another train for forty-five minutes. This rule would never fly, I thought to myself, and I was right.

Rule #36: Staff may attend wine industry events at the restaurant with approval from the wine director or head sommelier.

During our training, I had a lot of time to observe different departments. The pastry department was the most alternative, with their punky haircuts and multiple piercings. But the wine team was having the most fun. While management seemed quite serious, Paul Roberts commanded a corner of the room with his three underlings where there always seemed to be a joke afoot. I had always thought of sommeliers as stuffy, old, and—usually—French, but this crew seemed to be the antithesis. I made a mental note to take them up on this rule in the future.

AFTER READING ALL these rules, I began to think about my cornets and wondered if this was one of those times in life when it is important to play by the rules. Making soufflés and taking a driver's test were examples of such times—not that I had attempted either. I would need patience and a decent mixing bowl before I would attempt to coax an egg white into stiffly peaking, and it would take a miracle to get me behind the wheel of a car. I had found one of the few places in the world where it is more convenient not to drive, and I saw no reason to inconvenience anyone, including myself.

When I told one of the chefs in the kitchen a few months later about my first attempt at cornet making, he asked how it had gone. I told him that I had originally figured I would make do with my regular spatula and wrap the cones around a spoon or something instead of buying a mold. At this he laughed out loud, wiped tears from his eyes, and went back to dicing his red onion.

So I decided to try to work things out with the cookbook, this time following it punctiliously. I considered inviting a guest or two, but figured I had better master the technique before I embarrassed myself. First, I took myself and my credit card to Williams-Sonoma, where I bought cornet molds ($15), an offset spatula ($12), and a Silpat ($25). These were vast improvements to the hummus container and baking pan. The process went much more smoothly this time, although I still had to make some adjustments in thickness and oven temperature (I lowered the 400-degree suggestion to 375). For every four rounds of batter I fit onto my Silpat, one or two turned into cornets. A few sagged before their next crisping stage in the oven; others crumbled after being crisped. One batch burned and one had to be rewarmed because they started snapping when I tried to roll them around the cornet mold. The book recommends working on the open door of your oven, to keep the batter warm enough to work with. So I knelt before the open oven, realizing that despite years of English classes, I could not recall a single poem by Sylvia Plath. I did about thirty cornets, using some of the batter from the previous session. At a baking time of eight to ten minutes each and an extensive molding operation, the forming stage took about two hours.

By the time I reached assembly, I had grown to hate my perky pink creations. I had picked up a pastry bag ($10) for the crème fraîche at Williams-Sonoma after the molding fiasco, not wanting to take a chance filling the cornets with the point of a knife as the book allows. There was no way I would risk fracturing any more of the remaining wafers. I spent two hours dicing the salmon and concocting the lemon oil for the tartare. I lacked the fine dicing technique that would have made a sharp tartare, but it seemed to be holding together. Miraculously, the red onion crème fraîche came out perfectly, with a tiny crunch of onion in silky, salty cream, but I taste-tested a few spoonfuls to be sure.

I do not own a specially designed silver Christofle cornet stand, nor do I have a butler on staff. Anticipating such short-comings, the book advises filling a bowl full of rock salt in order to prop up and serve the cones. I had no rock salt on hand and tried to make do with rice and lentils; I ended up with rice in my crème fraîche and salmon from a few decapitated cones strewn amid the legumes. I lost a few cornets by pinching them too tightly as I piped the filling. And by the time I had topped the last remaining cone, the first cones, much like myself, were drooping and looking a little forlorn.

At the French Laundry and, eventually, at Per Se, an army of cooks bakes the cornets in perfectly calibrated ovens and stores them carefully in plastic containers. On order, a few are placed in another special wooden holder as the crème fraîche is piped in. The army makes uniform little balls of perfectly diced salmon on which a food runner places a tiny piece of chive, which was cut earlier in the day by some eager young extern. The runner wraps each cone with a tiny paper napkin and places it perfectly upright in a silver tray, after which they sail away in the hand of an Armani-clad waiter.

Just about the only similarity between the above and my own adventure was the waiter, minus the Armani. Exhausted, I slumped down on the blue bar stool, the one place to sit in my tiny kitchen, and started flipping through the book again, soothed as I always was by the untouchable perfection of each photograph, but intimidated now by the thought of the expertise required for each dish. If the cornet preparation seemed daunting, the truffled egg was frightening. This party pleaser challenges the ambitious host with severing the top of an eggshell, cleaning the interior by removing the thin membrane that lines it, filling it with a white truffle-infused custard and a layer of black truffle ragout, and topping it with a double-sided potato chip. Said potato chip, which would have taken half the previous day to prepare, is made by slicing a sculpted potato on a mandolin ($160), placing a single chive between two chips and baking them. Once again, in the restaurant, there's a chef to perform each of the tasks.

Even if one were to forgo the more virtuosic dishes, I mused from my perch, it would be difficult to capture Chef Keller's law of diminishing returns, which is the foundation of the cookbook. The home cook, even one equipped with a willing spouse, a decent kitchen, and more talent than I, would be challenged to prepare so many courses *à la minute* for a dinner party without spending the whole night in the kitchen. As Chef Keller suggests in his book, one course might include five different preparations of pork (one such dish he calls "head to toe" because it uses all parts of the animal, snout to trotters). And yet, if one changes the portion size to allow for larger and fewer courses, one loses most of the magic. "For every course, there is a perfect quantity. Some courses must be small because of what they are: A quail egg is small. One is enough; two eggs would be redundant."

The thought of quickly poaching quail eggs, placing them on small soup spoons with the requisite smoked bacon (for a dish called Bacon and Eggs); running back to the kitchen to grab the oysters in a sabayon of pearl tapioca and spoon caviar on top; race back to rescue the agnolotti from the pot before they become gummy; sear the bass; carve the lamb; scoop the sorbet before it melts; and drizzle, dot, and sprinkle the dessert into shape left me breathless. A cook who could attempt such a feat would not only disappoint her guests by her absence from the table, but would amass a mountain of dirty dishes rivaled only by an equally high mountain of debt to the specialty food store (where she miraculously found rue for the bass and Japanese yuzu in abundance).

Just when you think you have found one dish to incorporate in a sensible party menu, you spot a final flourish that defeats you: a garnish of fried garlic chips, an infused thyme oil, an exotic herb salt. As Susie Heller, who tested all the recipes in the book, says in her introduction, "If the degree of difficulty of a dish exceeds your desire to make it, please remember that it's all right to do only part of the recipe. Most people, I'm guessing, will not try the pig's head preparation, but it would be a shame for anyone to miss the gribiche sauce that goes with it." In other words, feel free to dumb it down, but don't expect much.

I closed the book and slid it back onto the shelf. It wasn't just that I would be working restaurant hours and never cook, or that my kitchen couldn't fit a table, let alone more than one guest. I knew that I would never cook again from this book. Back to food porn it would be—look, don't touch, I thought. The *French Laundry Cookbook* sets up an unattainable model, but perhaps that is the allure. I flipped forward to the five-spice lobster again, knowing now that I would never butter-poach that lobster or sear the generous piece of foie gras. No, I would be perfectly content with the overly charred grilled cheese that I would make for dinner using the maligned ends of an aging loaf and questionable cheese. But I could still look.

• A TIP •

Please do not ask us what *else* we do.
This implies that (a) we shouldn't aspire to work in the restaurant business even if it makes us happy and financially stable, (b) that we have loads of time on our hands because ours is such an easy job, and (c) that we are not succeeding in another field.

• mosquitoes on toast •

WET PAINT AND newly laid carpet prevented us from fully exploring the dining room when we relocated to the restaurant from the Hudson Hotel. Instead, we stood on our toes and craned. A thick fireplace and chimney divided a wall of windows overlooking Central Park. On either side of the fireplace would soon stand four round, well-spaced tables. Another seven tables were to look over the dining room and across the park from a raised level, reached by four marble stairs in the center of the room. Through a wide doorway at the far end, a glass wall revealed a small private dining room. The party who reserved this sixteenth table might possibly have the best eight to ten seats in the city, with an unhindered view of the park. The doorway through which we peered stood closer to the front door, host stand, and second private dining room. Unlike much of the rest of the restaurant, that large, spare, windowless white room was nearly complete, which was why it had been chosen as the site of our training.

We spent half our days attending food seminars, in which the entire staff sat facing forward in long rows, learning about barrel-aged vinegar, heirloom ducks, and such. The rest of the day, the chefs acquainted themselves with the five-thousand-square-foot kitchen while the dining room staff stayed behind for service training.

In all sessions, instead of memorizing the information, our managers encouraged us to steep ourselves in it. Since the menu changed every day, and twice a day on the weekends, it was much more important, for example, to grasp that fish came before meat, which came before cheese, than to know whether the chef used Provençal or Tuscan olive oil. Eventually, we would come to know even this by the components in the dish, but for now, we needed the basics.

Steeping proved challenging as they handed out sheet upon sheet of facts: the sculptor and date of the statues visible from the window, the acreage of Central Park, the biography of the private dining director. Every piece of handcrafted furniture and imported linen or tile had a story. By the time they distributed the three-page sample menu, of which I understood thirty percent or so, I wanted to kneel on the floor—made of imported Italian bronze—and beg for mercy. But if we found this intimidating, imagine how it would be for the guest who hadn't gone through weeks of training. Per Se and the French Laundry take reservations sixty days in advance. That means that the guests have been anticipating the meal for two months before they walk in the front door. Have they dressed right? Will they use the correct spoon? Will they order the right wine? We had to understand this anxiety if we were to make them feel comfortable.

When it comes to channeling anxiety, I have always excelled. Until this point, I had not understood exactly what I would be doing as a backserver and found myself increasingly nervous. Let's review a typical meal. The guests walk through the sliding glass door into the restaurant, where they are met by a host or hostess and the maître d'. Once seated, their captain greets them, takes a cocktail or wine order, and brings them menus. The captain explains the menu, takes the order, sells and serves the wine with the help of the sommelier, makes sure they liked their food, and delivers the check at the end of the meal. Everything else is done by the backserver. The backserver pours the water, serves the bread, marks the table (meaning that he or she sets the silverware for any number of courses), helps clear each course, fetches glassware, removes empty glasses, and pretty much runs the station. Without a captain, the station might get swamped; without a backserver, it would sink. Tragically, he or she is practically invisible to the guest. It is a mindless and fairly thankless job, and although I would have taken almost any job to work at Per Se, I saw pretty quickly that it would grow dull. Even the food runners had more contact with the guest. They spent half their time watching the chefs plate the food and the rest of their time in the dining room, explaining the food. The only thing the backserver explained were the kinds of bread and butter—six to eight times a night.

My first real friend, another backserver named Patrick, had me laughing seconds after I sat down next to him. With his cherubic face and funny little tuft of blond hair that seemed to spring from his forehead, he looked barely seventeen. In fact, at twenty-three, he had already managed a well-known restaurant and now aspired to work in the wine department.

"I know I shouldn't be wearing all this aftershave," he whispered to me with an impish grin as I sat down, "but I figured it was better than smelling like a distillery."

As backservers, we handled table maintenance, so our training began with setting and clearing tables. The maître d's gave detailed demonstrations, after which we practiced, using mock tables manned by managers and peers. After each one of us performed the intricate ritual of serving and clearing, our audience critiqued us. One of us moved too slowly, another too fast; one raised the plate in front of the guest's face like a helicopter; another approached from behind and startled the guest; we forgot to serve the ladies first; we backhanded the guest, meaning we reached in front him, rather than around him.

Once we mastered the basics, the managers threw us curve balls. At one point, one of the maître d's moved close to Laura, the general manager, and took her hand. When the backserver arrived with their settings, he tried to slide the silverware unobtrusively beneath them. They immediately withdrew their hands.

"Do you see how you just interrupted us?" the maître d' pointed out. "Nothing is important enough to interrupt the guest." In this instance, the backserver should have set the knife and fork on the other side of the setting and left their hands in peace. In a similar vein, while we were instructed to pour water and wine from the right with our right hands, to avoid backhanding and crossing the guest, there were exceptions. Instead of interrupting two people in conversation, we should pour from the other side so as not to break their eye contact with an elbow or a bottle. Laura stressed something called "the bubble." Each table had an invisible bubble of personal space around it, of varying depth. It was our job to determine the boundaries of that space, so as to make the guest feel cared for but not cramped.

On my turn to practice clearing, I approached so the guests could see me coming, placed the silverware on one plate and slid it out from under the guest, careful not to bring it in front of her face, careful not to let my thumb venture over the edge of the dish, and then did the same for her dining partner. I thought I had done everything perfectly when one of the managers leaned to the floor and picked up a sauce spoon that he had intentionally dropped.

"You must know the markings so you know if something is missing," he explained.

One of the kitchen servers stood too close when serving the soup—or, more accurately, watered-down ketchup in a shallow bowl.

"I feel cramped," complained one of the managers. "I should not be able to smell you." Patrick caught my eye from across the room and winked.

Another kitchen server stood too far away, so he had to bend forward to place the plate before the guest, causing his rear end to jut out behind him.

"Imagine if I were sitting at the table behind you. What would I be seeing right now?" Laura asked him.

Everyone participated in captain training so we all had at least a grasp on every aspect of service. A captain's job mainly entailed navigating the guests through the different menus, an act we called spieling. Per Se would offer three menus when we opened: five courses of larger portions (a choice of first courses, fish, meat, cheese, and dessert), the nine-course chef's tasting menu, and a "tasting of vegetables." Captains needed to learn how to explain the differences between the menus and encourage guests to choose the chef's tasting menu without feeling pressured, limited, or overwhelmed. This was the menu that the restaurant did best and, unless there were serious dietary concerns, would be the most enjoyable for the guest.

We were to avoid using terms like *signature* or *chef's choice* because they favored certain dishes as opposed to the experience of the tasting menu. In general, words that were rote or clichéd were discouraged. "Bon appétit" and "enjoy" are fine the first time you hear them, but if the maître d', captain, back-server, and kitchen server tells you to enjoy every course for nine courses, you might also enjoy tripping their shiny, lace-up Lincoln Town Car shoes.

No first names, no flirting, no hands on the chairs, no touching the guest. Restaurant right-of-way: guest first, then hot food, then cold food.

Because the guests should never have to ask for anything, the rules stated that we drop the check before they had a chance to ask. This required the utmost sensitivity. If we had the sense that they wanted to linger, we might delay the check and let the maître d' know it might be a while. If they seemed to be in a hurry, we might deliver it right after the last cookies hit the table. In any case, we would leave it in the middle or toward the edge of the table without ceremony or comment. Mercifully, the rules also stated that the first guest to give a credit card would pay. Waiters despise when guests rope them into an argument over the check. Even in the two years that I had worked in the business, people had shoved cards in my pocket, pulled me back and forth, tried to corner me in the hallway, and even accused me of discrimination when it came to paying.

We discussed at length every movement made in the dining room, from the distance between our feet when we served each plate (six inches) to the level at which to carry the plates (just above the waist with elbows at right angles). While I found myself overwhelmed at first, wondering if I should ask how to walk and breathe as well, I saw a reason behind everything we learned, namely how to put the guest at ease.

But there was one arena in which I could not imagine ever being at ease: wine. "Striped bass with ginger vinaigrette. What do you serve?"

Red with meat, white with fish, I thought to myself as hands shot up across the room, mine not one of them.

"I'm thinking an Alsatian white or a Swiss Chasselas," answered one of the captains whom I had overheard talking about his two previous jobs at four-star restaurants.

Chasse-what?

Paul Roberts, the wine director, taught most of our wine seminars, flanked by three minions: a foppish blond with horn-rimmed glasses and two black men, both of average height, both with shiny bald heads and spaces between their teeth. At the French Laundry, they had fun with the fact that people mistook them, pocketing the other's tips, switching tables to see if anyone noticed. Their walks, I discovered, defined them. One walked a little like a penguin. The other, André, had this bowlegged glide that, when in jeans and round-toed sneakers, made him look a little like Ernie; in a pinstriped suit, his walk had an irresistibly quirky charm.

Paul must have had all the sommeliers go up there and introduce themselves, but I only remember André. He wore a checkered shirt that reminded me of the very picnic blanket I was soon daydreaming of putting into a picnic basket with some very rare roast beef and unpronounceable cheese. He could bring the Chasselas and, while he was at it, maybe explain what it was. In my limited experience with sommeliers, I had learned to dread the tedious dictums on chalky soil and the supposed happenings on my midpalate. But this wine team, and André in particular, had an inventive way of talking about the subject. I liked that he called wine "bangin'," described bottles as "Victoria's Secret" (silky, lacy, and seductive), and claimed to smell lathered ponies. He had two different wine keys, labeled "Chocolate Mousse" and "Bad Mo Fo."

By the time I refocused, he was talking about how he began his career in Texas, in such esteemed establishments as McDonald's and Red Lobster. I began to pay better attention. So far I had met a bunch of New York career waiters who knew they knew it all, a crew of culinary school graduates who had recently been told that they knew it all, and a few like myself who were keeping quiet because we knew we knew very little. André fit into none of these categories. Here he was: from Texas, the land of meat and tequila, a black man in a world of old, white, wine-swirling men, with a résumé that could be held against him. Anticipating the question in my head, he explained briefly that he became interested in wine as a means to boost his check average as a waiter, but I suspected that there was more to the story. After a few months of intensive reading on his own, he decided to test his own knowledge and entered a wine competition. He won. And then he won again. And then he went to the nationals in Miami and won again. At this point he approached Paul Roberts, the only Master Sommelier in Texas, the highest ranking for wine service professionals, and told him he wanted a job. It just so happened that Paul was moving to California to work at the French Laundry, and eventually to open Per Se, and he needed to hire a few sommeliers for the new place. Could André be in California in a few weeks to begin training? He was.

A few days into orientation, some of the female backservers, runners, and chefs were down in the women's locker room trying on uniforms and lamenting about buffable black lace-up shoes.

"Who's the sexy sommelier?" I asked, although it was clear

by my tone that I knew perfectly well who he was and was doing a little homework.

"That's my boyfriend," I heard over my shoulder and turned to see that it was Leigh, one of the women I had seen working behind the bar. "Of seven years."

Oops. Oh well, there were a few others I had my eye on.

The only profession to which I would liken the restaurant dating scene would be the theater. The romance with the co-star/coworker ends when the play ends or when the waiter moves to a different restaurant. Then it's on to the next play or restaurant and another crew of beautiful, young, and restless actors with too much time on their hands and career aspirations easily put on hold for another beer or six. My first job, as a busser, came through that childhood sweetheart I told you about—he left me for his costar. Our first kiss, at age seventeen, had taken place while making oatmeal-raisin cookies. From then on, most of my affairs were related to food in one way or another. There was the Mexican sous chef who seduced me at Coney Island, after hot dogs and a six-pack of Corona. Next up was a relationship with a food runner based entirely on lunches at restaurants we couldn't afford for dinner. He was very sweet and very attractive, but he was also a Republican ex-marine who watched football on television. That didn't work for about four reasons.

After working with a bunch of artists who lived on ramen noodles, I was feeling like a very small fish at Per Se—a white sardine, maybe. Half the staff had come from the French Laundry for a few months to help us open the restaurant. To me, this meant that, though they were quite friendly, they knew everything and were, therefore, intimidating. Miraculously, and I say this having barely survived the vicious cliques of Edmunds Middle School, I became friendly with a few of the Californians. After training, we began migrating over to Kennedy's, an Irish pub around the corner. Later, we moved to the Coliseum, which was half a block closer (and after seventy hours a week on your feet, this makes a difference) and became a sort of petri dish for anything brewing. Or, in many cases, for anything breeding.

The camaraderie was a little distracting for some of us, but it also helped us work together. When service flowed seamlessly, we called it "the dance." In these moments, there was a grace to our movements, a sense of poise, an awareness of our bodies in relation to one another and to our guests. In the months of training for this restaurant's opening, we not only learned glassware series and the names of the cows that produced the milk from which our butter was made, but were coached by an eighteenth-century dance specialist. One afternoon, at the Hudson Hotel, we learned to walk, to stand, and to bow like ladies and gentlemen. Ladies were taught to look demure and to curtsy. Gentlemen learned to stand with one foot ahead of the other and the opposite hand on imaginary sword hilts. It seemed absurd at the time, but in fact much of it came in handy. When holding two hot plates of Snake River Farms calotte de boeuf with crispy bone marrow and a rissole of marble potatoes, one was wise to hold them close to the center of gravity, learned in curtsy training, so as not to make the marble potatoes roll around the plate like their namesakes.

Toward the end of that session at the Hudson, our instructor split us into two long lines and took out a bouquet of multicolored feathers.

"I would normally give the feathers to the ladies," she explained as she passed them out, "but we will have to make do." Out of fifty or so front-of-the-house employees present, there were maybe six or seven women.

"The point of this dance is to think about giving and receiving," she said, pressing play on her tiny boom box. A slow and stately march started playing through tinny speakers, a march to which we learned a simple dance: stepping up to our partner to give him the feather, stepping back to a bow, taking his hand, turning around, receiving the feather again, and stepping back to the line.

"Are you starting to feel each other's sense of space?" she called out. Someone sneezed.

As the dance went on, we grew more comfortable with one another, roughhousing and fighting over the props.

"I've been defeathered!"

"Giveth the feather backeth or I will have to unsheathe my sword!"

WHEN WE OPENED the restaurant, we were armed with wine keys and Mont Blanc pens instead of feathers and fantasy swords, but we were going to need more than these to survive on the dining room floor. We also had the menu and the wine list to contend with.

Let's say two guests, Mr. and Mrs. Bichalot, have just been seated on table five, which is restaurant-speak for sitting at table five, and have chosen the chef's tasting menu. Hopefully they took our suggestion of champagne in anticipation of the first course, a rich caviar preparation called Oysters and Pearls. Expecting the dish to stand up to scotch or something equally palate-dulling is expecting a great deal from a fish egg. The Bichalots critique the flowers (quite *tall*, don't you think?) and the view (it's a pity Chef Keller didn't choose a higher floor), the sparseness of the walls (Darling, perhaps a loan of a little artwork is in order?), until a waiter appears on their left with something they hadn't considered for years: an ice cream cone. At that point, they relax and begin to take the whole affair a little less seriously, because, amid all this marble and ritual, someone has done something *rather* clever.

Being well acquainted with the salmon cornet at this point, you would gobble that thing down in the recommended two to three bites, which optimally, combine the cone, the crème fraîche, and the salmon. Mr. and Mrs. Bichalot, however, are "challenged," as the backservers call anyone who would eat an ice cream cone with a knife and a fork. Now their table must be reset with new silverware and plates and possibly even a new bread plate if they have left the paper or a cornet tip there. They might even need to be crumbed if they have scattered sesame seeds or cornet shards on the tablecloth. Being cornet-challenged is the first sign of danger to a backserver. The next thing you know, they will be asking for half-still, half-sparkling water, wanting the blinds lowered midsunset, and suddenly becoming a vegetarian when the first meat course arrives.

The Bichalots, having finished ravaging their cornets, are now crumbed and set with mother-of-pearl spoons, with which they will eat their caviar. "What a relief," Mrs. Bichalot confides to Mr. Bichalot—metal implements, as they well know, can cause caviar to taste a little tinny. Mr. and Mrs. Bichalot are moving on to caviar because it is the next course of their tasting menu. If, however, the chef decides to give them VIP treatment (for example, if Mr. Bichalot's nephew was the sous chef's mother's sister's neighbor's stockbroker, or if they were in the restaurant business themselves, or employees of Per Se or the French Laundry, or a major newscaster or politician), they will have only just begun their canapé experience when their grumbling backserver crumbed their table (with an Italian sterling silver crumber that looks a little like a razor clam).

Sometimes the kitchen will give each guest at the table a different version of the same dish, four different canapé-sized soups or sorbets, for example. Other times they will give two guests one thing and two guests another, or any other configuration that would make things exciting for a larger party. (There is a term for this at the restaurant, but if I tell you, you might go in and ask for it and I would get in trouble. Extra canapés are a gift from the chef and to ask for them, even if you are willing to pay, would be like calling a dinner guest and telling them that instead of a bottle of wine or some flowers, you would like them to weave you a new tablecloth. Please don't do this.)

Here is a possible sequence of VIP canapés:

1. **SOUP**: Some are clear consommés, some simple purees, others more complex veloutés and foams.

2. **SAVORY SORBETS** (in warmer months): These might be beet, basil, red pepper, cilantro, or even a fruit like yuzu paired with Molokai salt, a black salt from Hawaii.

3. **CAVIAR**: Oysters and Pearls is the restaurant's most famous caviar preparation, but one might see caviar on a potato blini, cauliflower panna cotta, pickled oysters, apple granita, or avocado mousse with pistachio oil.

4. **COLD FISH**: This really depends on the season and could be anything from a crab claw to sea urchin.

5. **HOT FISH**: Again, the possibilities are endless. If there isn't also a tempura canapé course, tempura is a possibility, but so is a turbot cheek or a salmon chop (that one's in the cookbook).

6. **CUSTARD**: No matter the VIP, there will certainly

be a course devoted solely to *eggs and truffles*:
custards with truffle ragout, eggs scrambled
with truffle coulis or coddled with truffle beurre
noisette. My favorite, the deviled egg with a truffle
"Pop-Tart," looks exactly like the picnic food and
toaster treat except that the pastry is filled with a
marmalade of Périgord truffles and drizzled with
truffle frosting.

7. **MEAT**: The kitchen has a lot of fun with this
course, wrapping aged beef around fried bone
marrow, frying up some quail wings, or braising
a little cockscomb. If the restaurant knows that
a guest likes offal, most likely this is where
she will get her sweetbreads or brains.

In order to understand the sequence of VIP canapés, we
were taught a little etymology 101. At the French Laundry and
Per Se, the whole range of amuse-bouches (literally translat-
ing to "mouth amusers"), from soups to blini, is referred to as
canapés. This is, however, not technically accurate. The word
canapé comes from the French word for couch, and actually refers to the specific practice of resting a savory topping on a
piece of toast or cracker like Mr. Bichalot's slippered feet on
his chaise longue, only infinitely more savory.

The word can be traced by an alternate route to the Greek
konops, meaning "mosquito." Having yet discovered the joys of
DDT, the Greeks hung netting called *konopion* around their beds
and couches to protect themselves from the *konops*, a technique
that was later adopted by the Romans. They called the curtains
conopeum, which became the Latin *canopeum*, the Middle English *canope*, and eventually "canopy." How the French came to
use *canapé* to refer to a couch instead of a curtain is beyond the

limits of my steepability, but we have stolen the word for use in Modern English and retained its Middle English meaning.

Upon further research (I know, I know), I learned that traditional canapés begin with a bread base, usually measuring one-eighth to one-quarter inch in thickness, shaped in a triangle, round, or strip, and fried, sautéed, or toasted to add crunch. They should be able to be eaten in less than three bites, although one bite is preferable for standing hors d'oeuvres, and should not be so brittle as to crumble on haute couture.

Tell Mr. and Mrs. Bichalot that I'll be right there.

Canapés trespass upon an array of different traditions. Broadly, they fall under the heading of hors d'oeuvres, an eighteenth-century French term later used to describe cuisines from other nations as well, meaning "outside the work" or out of the ordinary course of things, much like this little tangent of mine. Usually hors d'oeuvres are served at the opening of a meal, as a means of whetting the appetite. Canapés have different guises in different cultures, from the Italian crostini or bruschetta to Chinese dim sum. The English call their version *savories*, although they have fallen a bit out of fashion since the eighteenth century, like the English themselves, when they were served before or instead of dessert (the savories, not the English), where a cheese course falls in French cuisine. One English recipe from 1759 features anchovy fillets on fried bread fingers with Parmesan and Seville orange juice. Later, in the nineteenth and twentieth centuries, small savories took on fanciful names such as "angels on horseback" (fried oysters wrapped in bacon and served on fried bread slices). British savories exist today in what food historian Alan Davidson calls in the *Oxford Companion to Food* the "time warp" of London clubs and nostalgic restaurants.

I will admit that some of that research I did on my own, but the majority of it came from materials we were given at Per Se. Despite the serious curriculum, however, Chef Keller made it clear that he did not take himself or his food too seriously, "This is not religion. It is food," he said in one of our training sessions. Or, as another friend in the business once said, it's just chicken under a tree. The whimsical tone set with the salmon cornet continues throughout the meal. Before you have a chance to truly mourn the passing of the cornet, the Oysters and Pearls arrives. Butter-poached oysters (usually Island Creek, Bagaduce, or Malpec, depending on availability) swim in a creamy sabayon of pearl tapioca and are heaped generously with caviar (Iranian osetra, Russian sevruga, or American). The courses that follow maintain a playful and ironic bent. Macaroni and Cheese is a cute name for lobster with mascarpone-enriched orzo pasta. Soup and a Sandwich features a seasonal soup and a tiny brioche sandwich with shaved black truffles inside.

For the most part, after the meat canapé, VIPs begin to follow a path similar to their fellow diners. As you observed earlier, Mr. and Mrs. Bichalot moved from the salmon cornet to Oysters and Pearls. At this point, they proceed to the salad or foie gras course. Mr. Bichalot really shouldn't because of his cholesterol—still, he supposes just this once a little foie gras won't hurt, but Mrs. Bichalot finds liver of all kinds repulsive, so she will go with the salad of hearts of palm with truffle coulis. This will be followed by a swimming fish. Next is a lobster course, although between November and April you might find scallops. The first meat course is usually a light meat such as quail, rabbit, duck, or pork, while the second meat course features a fuller meat, often beef, lamb, or veal, usually roasted, grilled, or braised. The composed cheese course, a piece of art on a plate, precedes sorbet and, finally, dessert. Well, almost finally. The mignardises that follow are completely optional: tiny pots de crème and crème brûlée, shortbread, macaroons, and chocolate truffles.

During the course of this menu, not only were we to seamlessly set, or mark, the table, serve the food, explain to the guests what they were about to eat, and clear the plates so as to keep the pace without rushing the guest, but we often had to drizzle, shave, grate, or ladle some final touch onto the dish. Luckily we had an entire seminar devoted to condiments.

At some restaurants, this would be a quick seminar: the canapé might be crabmeat on a piece of toast with an Asian vinaigrette and a sprig of something green; pepper, olive oil, and slices of lemon upon request would be the extent of the condiments. Not so at Per Se. Chef Keller used things like salt and lemon to intensify flavor, but thought of artisanal oils and vinegars as condiments that should be offered to the guest at the table by a server who appreciated the product. We tasted and discussed French and Italian olive oils (because the French pick their olives later in the season, French olive oil tends to be rounder and sweeter while Italian oil is often a little spicier). We learned the difference between forced infusion done in the kitchen for something like the thyme oil often paired with lamb and oils infused with, say, lemon zest, at the press. Tasting Armando Manni's olive oil from Tuscany led to a discussion of the effect of air, light, and temperature on the oil. By packing his two oils (Per Me and Per Mio Figlio) in small, dark anti-UV bottles marked with their vintage, Manni preserves more of the beneficial phenols in his oil that are usually lost in generic oils. We also tasted banyuls, truffles, and twenty-year aged balsamic vinegars.

Was this overkill? If we were simply learning the ingredients in the kitchen, I might have said so. But if I was going to be serving one-hundred-year vinegar drip by drip from a silver spoon onto the plates of restaurant critics and movie stars, I wanted to know exactly what I was dripping. And this was just the beginning of the day's seminar. When it came to canapés, we had theory to learn before we even got to the practical.

Deep in the trenches of training, I was still following and taking copious notes, which I would attempt to commit to memory when no one was looking. I understood why dishes on the menu increased in weight and size from, say a caviar preparation in the beginning to braised pork shoulder later in the menu, but when put on the spot I still wasn't sure into which meat course veal or duck would fall or why cold foie gras preparations were offered with the salad course while hot foie gras took the place of the first meat course. Some of it I would just have to trust I would get eventually, but there were a few tricks as well.

It should say something about the depth of knowledge in every department that Paul Roberts, the wine director, initially outlined the menu for us—and not Chef Keller or even the maître d'. When it came to cheeses, most of us would admit, if only to ourselves, that we were lost. If you had asked me the difference between Cabacou and Chabichou, I would have suggested calling the whole thing off.

"Repeat after me," Paul instructed us. "Goat, cow, sheep, blue."

"Goat, cow, sheep, blue," we echoed back once, then again, and then again.

Paul conducted from the front of the room with an imaginary baton I pictured as a breadstick. By George, it seemed we'd got it. If a guest ever pointed to a cheese and for the life us we couldn't remember if it was raw or pasteurized, washed rind or wrapped in hoja santa leaves, all we had to do was think to ourselves, goat, cow, sheep, blue, for they were always listed in that order. Then at least we would have one thing to say about the cheese before we ran to the back to look it up.

During the course of menu training, we had guest speakers discuss heritage birds and wild mushrooms, the difference between Iranian and Russian caviar, and the ideal brewing techniques for black, green, and white tea. But even more inspiring were the times when cooks from a certain department sat at the front of the room and explained how they got there and how they did their jobs. Generally, young chefs don't have much chance to address crowds and Thomas often had to coach them with leading questions. I had already noticed that in Chef Keller's kitchens, everyone was called "chef," not only The Chef. In fact, everyone who worked in the restaurant, from the reservationists to the coffee server, was called "chef." It was an equalizer, a sign of respect for people's métiers, and a great way to get out of learning hundreds of co-workers' names. Not that Thomas didn't know our names, because, for the most part, he did. It was surprisingly hard to resist, and I was soon calling my mother "chef," as well as cab-drivers and guests. I even fell into the habit of calling friends "chefie," which even I found irritating. Once, when I called a man I was dating "chef," he became irate.

"Who's Jeff?" he demanded. When I tried to explain that I had actually called him "chef," he looked dubious.

"I bet you know who this Jeff is, you little Judas," he said to the dog sitting at the end of the bed—whom I regularly called "chef" as well.

For the people in my life who still didn't appreciate the intensity of this training, I simply explained that one day we tasted nine different salts and another day we tasted sixteen kinds of chocolate. This was impressive, but there was one final piece to the menu that blew my mind. At Per Se and the French Laundry, there is no repetition of ingredients on a guest's menu, besides luxuries such as truffles and foie gras. If there were almonds on the pompano, the pastry department would have to skip the almond milk sorbet they were so excited about. If, in the dead of winter, when fruit options are already limited, there was grapefruit on the salad, that was off limits for other dishes as well. When I heard this, I began to understand the true virtuosity of the menu. I also pitied the chefs. One of them, who worked cheese, told me that at the end of the night, when all the chefs gathered to plan the next day's menu, he always had the perfect accompaniments in mind for certain cheeses. Let's say he was planning a carrot slaw and pickled dates. The fish chef de partie claimed peas and carrots for the lobster prep, the meat chef de partie wanted dates with the lamb, and by the time they got to cheese, the poor chef was on plan D. I felt for him, but I had once been served a tasting menu at a wonderful restaurant specializing in seasonal produce during spring. There had been asparagus in literally every dish. I love asparagus, but after chilled asparagus soup, fiddlehead and asparagus salad, and saddle of rabbit with sautéed asparagus, I was tired of it.

I am certain that Mr. and Mrs. Bichalot, on the other hand, were far from bored. They had a few words about the apathetic motion sensor at the bathroom sink and the lack of black napkins for those in black suits and the fact that they had to wait on the phone for hours to get a reservation and that the sliding front door was hard to figure out and that there are too many quotation marks in the menu, but other than that it was fabulous. The maître d' showed them out, the backserver swooped in with a large silver tray to load the remaining dishes, and the coffee servers followed with a freshly pressed tablecloth.

In a few moments, table five would be reset and another party would be ready to be told about the choices of water and bread and to receive their salmon cornets.

Somewhere toward the end of our training, just as I was beginning to feel comfortable, we were ushered into a conference room and given the first of what would be many tests. So much for steeping. Questions ranged from the difference between black and summer truffles, the grape in Vouvray, whether we brown the bones for veal stock, the definition of *glaçage*, and my favorite—which I still can't answer: "Circle the correct ONE: Cippolini, Cipolini, Cipollini, Cipolinni."

I got every one of the above wrong, but that last one was a cruel and unusual question, so it doesn't count.

• A TIP •

Please enable us to give you what you ordered by
making enough space for it. There should be at least
ten inches in front of you that are free of:
hands
elbows
silverware
bread plates
teacups
wineglasses
and ample bosoms

————

• fire! •

————

bETWEEN TRAINING AND opening night, we suited up
for a purgatorial period known as the "soft opening"
or "friends-and-family." In theory, this grace period would allow us to work out any kinks in our service. In actuality, our
guinea pigs were the most informed and critical of all possible
guests: members of the press, celebrities, French Laundry regulars, managers' and chefs' spouses, and our peers, who knew
better than anyone just how badly we blundered.

Our first encounter with the public took place on February 4: a black-tie opening gala for the $1.8 billion, 2.8 million-
square-foot Time Warner Center. In the hype, there were even
rumors that the president might grace us with his presence.
He didn't show, but we were not wanting for fame and for-
tune. Politicians, newscasters, designers, actors, opera sing-
ers, rappers, authors, and business tycoons strolled through
the vertical urban retail project (mall), while Cirque du Soleil
performed in the vaulted glass lobby.

It just so happened that the party coincided with the strapless glitz of New York's Fashion Week. Trays of champagne flutes were enveloped by throngs of women with blinding jewels and men with blindingly white teeth. Trays of pastry, however, caused the same crowds to recoil. I found myself bristling at this reception, not because we servers were ignored—holding a tray hardly deserved flattery—but because our guests seemed not to notice the food, the room, or even the view. When I passed Patrick, my backserver friend, on my way to the kitchen to secure a single spoon of salmon tartare for a woman "allergic" to dairy, wheat, and refined sugar, we paused for a moment at the window to look at the moon. It loomed over the park like a gold coin.

Later in the week, a famous comedian booked the restaurant for a private party, to which he invited one hundred of his closest friends. When we learned in the preshift meeting that, due to a serious allergy, the host requested there be no truffles on the menu, Patrick leaned over and whispered, "What percentage of the population even *knows* it's allergic to truffles?" He and I were on canapé duty, passing tiny cups of curried cauliflower soup, applewood-smoked bacon popcorn, and bonito-wasabi Rice Krispie treats.

By the end of the week, I was tired of holding trays and repeating "Salmon cornet with red onion crème fraîche?" (Although, offering salmon to a famous author quite similarly named was a highlight of the week. I approached him anxiously chanting "sammen, sammen, sammen" under my breath so as to be sure I didn't pronounce the *l* by mistake.) I was ready to put down my trays of canapés and start serving some real food, but I had no idea what I was in for.

The first night of mock service, we had one seating and one menu, but the pace dragged and our poor friends and family

were held at the tables for hours, the jury of a particularly tedious trial. The pace improved on the second night, but this
time it was our turn to suffer. If our experience was anything
like that of the French Laundry, the majority of our guests
would choose the chef's tasting menu, with or without our encouragement. It seemed to me that if one wanted large portions and fewer courses, there were hundreds of restaurants
around the city that excelled in such a menu. What we did
well was the tasting menu, with its diverse flavors that were
designed to flow in a certain order. Still, for whatever reason,
the management decided to offer a menu with larger portions
when we opened. And on the second day of friends-and-family,
they thought it would be good practice to serve only five-course
menus.

The worst order for the backserver, the kitchen, and, argu-
ably, the guests, was one that mixed and matched from all the
menus. Instead of all having the same fish course (fish fork,
fish knife, and sauce spoon for everyone), one guest would have
the fish from the chef's tasting (fish gear), one would have the
jícama salad from the tasting of vegetables (small fork, small
knife), one would have nothing in front of him because he had
ordered the five-course menu (silverware and a show plate),
and one guest, who ordered the chef's tasting but didn't like
fish, would have something like pasta (small fork, small knife,
spoon). It was a nightmare for the restaurant and an alienat-
ing dining experience for the guests.

So, when the management decided to offer only five-course
menus on our second night of service, we knew we were going
down. Even though we thought we had everything planned
out, we discovered many an unaddressed issue even before the
service began. Where were the butter knives? Could we leave
the butter out or did it need to remain in the refrigerator?

Wouldn't it be too cold? How much water needed to be stocked for us to get through the night? Was it against health regulations to keep the ice scoop in the ice bin?

By the second course, our training had gone out the window; this service was about survival, not finesse. I kept my cheat sheet with all the markings in my silverware drawer, but was still confused when I reached the table. Was it soup, soup, salad, pasta or salad, soup, pasta, soup? Meanwhile, we were out of forks and had to run to the dish station and polish more as our tables went without bread and water and made a mental note to report this oversight to whomever had invited them.

In the restaurant business, we have a term for being so busy that professionalism, patience, and grace turns to hysterical, humorless chaos. We call it being in the weeds. The night of five-course hell was my first experience with being truly in the weeds at Per Se. I had just caught up with my marking and was about to offer more bread to some guests who had asked for it about two courses before, when my captain cut his eyes over to a table that needed to be cleared. I put down the breadbasket, cursing him under my breath. When we rounded the corner, out of view of the dining room, he piled his plates on mine, saying he needed to be in the station at all times. To what? Go butter up the general manager's wife or top off full glasses of wine? I stormed into the dish room, slammed the plates down, and began to hurl each piece of silverware into its designated soapy bin.

"Slow down, Chef," said a quiet voice to my right.

It was Chef Keller. Apparently, he had stepped in to relieve the dishwasher, who had also found himself in the weeds. I had just enough time to be mortified before sprinting back to my station to assess the damage. Chef Keller subsequently flew the head dishwasher from the French Laundry to New York to train the new team.

For the most part, the excitement of the opening distracted me from how exhausted and anxious I was. I barely noticed sweating in my boxy suit, the noose around my neck, or the fact that I hadn't had a chance to go to the bathroom in about six hours. On some weeks, I had two days off, one for school and one for sleep. But just as often, my school day was my one day off. Luckily, we had a night of pampering built into the pandemonium.

Each of us had what many New Yorkers would kill for: a reservation at Per Se. Over the course of two evenings, the managers assigned each employee a party and time and instructed him to show up in proper attire. The staff was divided in two; while one half dined, the other half worked. I was on the floor for the first service and had Paul Roberts in my section, meaning that the pressure was off and we all had a good time. The following night, I lucked out again. In my party of six sat one of the maître d's, and we were given VIP treatment. Thankfully, I took notes during and after the meal, because, with a wine per course, I never would have remembered anything after the first six canapés. I put stars next to the dishes that I loved: the Oysters and Pearls (a sentiment shared by most of the guests in my future), the lobster with English pea coulis and morels, and the degustation of lamb, featuring the braised shoulder and roasted saddle, fava beans, and chanterelles. On a separate page, I recorded my observations with many an exclamation point.

Repetition! The fish knife doesn't cut!! (It seemed my exclamation points increased with my wine intake.) André rocks!!!

After the parties, the friends-and-family dinners, and the staff-on-staff meals, we were ready to get to work. It would be a relief to serve the kind of guest willing to listen to the reservation recording loop for hours. And it was. I loved their questions about the preparations of dishes, the ingredients, our staff, the fireplace—all of which I was relieved to be able to answer. No one asked the square footage of Central Park. As the first real week drew to an end, I genuinely looked forward to my future with the restaurant.

ON OUR FIRST Saturday night, chefs hurriedly finished their mise en place for the busy service; captains, having ironed the linen and set the tables, debated wine pairings; kitchen servers practiced "spieling" the foie gras course. I entered a heated discussion with Patrick regarding what silverware to use for the potage parmentier. Technically it was a soup and should require only a spoon, but Patrick thought the crisp Princess La Ratte potato slices called for a knife, which, for the sake of symmetry, we agreed would mean a fork as well.

"Is it smoky in here?" someone asked casually. This sent a few elbows into the ribs of Michael, the ex-cook and current captain whose six years with the company had earned him the privilege of tending the fireplace in the dining room. He shared the duty with the male maître d's and managers who competed silently among themselves to see whose fire was the biggest. After one added a log, another went by to prod it.

"Now that's a fire," I heard muttered on more than one occasion.

I gathered during training that Per Se's fireplace had required intense lobbying, being the first to have been allowed in a Manhattan commercial space in years. The extensive politicking must have been worth it to Chef Keller, who wanted to bring the homey touch of the French Laundry to the city.

He had already traded an herb garden for Central Park and a small wooden house for thirteen thousand square feet in the Time Warner Building; his share alone was rumored to have cost twelve million dollars. Per Se housed other elements from the French Laundry, namely the blue front doors, accents of Australian oak, similar menus, and much of his California staff, but the fireplace was the heart of the dining room.

Michael told me later that when he began to smell smoke, he walked to the offices in the back where the managers were having a meeting. "Thomas, there's a bunch of smoke in the restaurant," he remembers saying. For the moment, their attention was focused on that night's service. After the week of fashionistas came a wave of gossip-prone foodies and press ravenous for a review. It was no wonder that management was distracted from the smoke now pouring into the restaurant. Only after another employee rushed in to deliver the same news did they follow Michael toward the dining room.

There was no need to see the dining room, however, because one look made it clear that the smoke was not coming from the fireplace, but rather from the wall behind the fish butcher's station. Someone called the fire department, and the managers turned their attention to getting everyone out. They first ushered us into the hallway connecting the back of the restaurant to the fourth floor of the Time Warner shops. Ignorant of the source of the fire, we suspected fireplace complications or a burned loaf of brioche, and resumed testing one another on the tea list and rehearsed spieling "torchon of foie gras with spiced winter fruits" and "tentation au chocolat, noisette, et lait."

"What are the winter fruits again?" asked one of the runners.

"Apricots, dates, apples, figs."

"And, Julio. Don't forget that fruit!"

"Very funny," said Julio.

After a few minutes in the hall, one of the managers came through the doors and announced that we should proceed calmly down to the first floor. Chefs, in their royal blue aprons, and waiters, in their black suits, filled all three escalators, but only a few pairs of eyes looked up through the bookstore window. Quite a number of well-clad shoppers stopped to inquire about reservations, but on the whole, New Yorkers did what they do to anything out of the ordinary: they walked right by. There's a reason the naked cowboy spends his days in tourist-filled Times Square—he would be ignored anywhere else in the city. As there was no alarm and the fire engines had yet to arrive, the collection of culinary professionals gathered in front of Williams-Sonoma looked more like participants in a massive cooking demo than victims of a fire. Only when the fire department pulled up did reality hit us.

"Do you think I have time to get a smoothie?"

"There is no way we will open tonight."

"Shit, I left my stuff in coat check."

"I bet you T.K. will want to go down with the ship," joked one of the captains brought in from the French Laundry. "This whole building will go up in flames and he'll have to be dragged from the kitchen."

That caused a few laughs and nods, but the group was growing more serious. People began looking around to make sure everyone was there.

"Where's Michael?"

As it turned out, Michael, who had been worried that his overenthusiastic use of kindling had indeed been the cause of the fire, stayed in the restaurant to see what he could do. The French Laundry captain had been right: Chef Keller refused to leave the kitchen. As the air filled with smoke, he stood at the heavy stainless-steel table in the center of the kitchen, known as the pass. In service, this is where the commanding chef and his sous chefs called out the orders and plated the food. The pass was the front line; on one side was an army of cooks, on the other an army of servers. If something went wrong on either side, this is where things turned ugly. At this moment, however, things had truly turned ugly. "Per Se's on fire," Chef Keller supposedly reported over and over into his cell phone, pausing only to swear and redial. He only put away the phone when a fireman climbed up on his $250,000 stove and raised an ax over his head.

"That moment will be frozen in my mind forever," Chef Keller later recalled in an all-staff meeting. The fireman had stood there, waiting for the sign from the chief, the chef explained. When the ax came down on the wall and flames leaped out, he knew that this wasn't going to be a minor setback.

For those of us who had been waiting downstairs, the news of the evening's closure was like the phone call on a snow day. We headed back up the escalator to retrieve our belongings, which were safe in the locker room on the second floor. Not knowing the extent of the damage or what it would mean to our lives and our paychecks, it was agreed that the best thing for everyone would be to head across the street for a beer.

At the staff meeting days later, we were instructed not to leave town because the restaurant could open any day. So for ten weeks, those who paid any attention to that commandment puttered around the city. Some of the chefs spent time in other restaurants' kitchens, refining their techniques. The reservationists found guests reservations at other restaurants or rescheduled their Per Se reservations. The dining room staff underwent a correspondence course of sorts, involving daily testing. But this required only so much time, so most of us took on other challenges. Some found temporary jobs, others took classes. I skipped town for a long weekend and then embarked on a series of disastrous affairs.

MY BROTHER, SAM, and my sister-in-law had just delivered their first baby, and I doubted that a chance to meet her would present itself again once the restaurant reopened, so I called my family in Vermont and announced that I would be there in a few days. When my mother picked me up at the airport, she seemed distracted, but I chalked it up to being a new grandmother. When she dropped me off at the bottom of my brother's snowy driveway, I began to get suspicious. My father was waiting for me inside the house. After a quick introduction to the tiny and perfect Sophie, my father announced that, after thirty years, he and my mother were splitting up. Was there someone else? I wanted to know. There was. As soon as my father left, my mother came back, making it to the top of the driveway this time. She cried; my brother, Sam, cried; Sophie cried in solidarity; and I did what I always do in a crisis: I looked into dinner.

"I feel like one family is beginning and another is ending," Sam confided later that night as we cleaned up the kitchen. He made us Whiskey Sours, which are among his greatest gifts to the world, after genius photographs and peerless eggs Benedict.

"At least you have a family," I responded bitterly.

My memory of that whole weekend is blurry, most likely because I didn't let the reality of my parents' divorce sink in until I was safe at home. I had been feeling less and less like their home was my own, but this confirmed it. I couldn't wait to get back to New York. At least there I could count on tenant rights and the fact that no one could take my sunny studio away from me. This was the first time I had truly lived alone, and I was fiercely attached to my apartment. I was the one who monitored the thermostat and let the dishes stack up and left the screens open. For some reason, just knowing that my name was in the phone book in Brooklyn made me feel like I had an official place in the universe.

When I returned to the city, I resumed my life with a new level of attention, as if I were observing it before crawling into my own skin. I savored my morning coffee ritual, grinding the beans, heating and steaming the milk, and prewarming my wide blue mug before settling in to the corner of my couch. Mornings were my own, the only sounds being the temperamental toilet whose handle liked to be just so, and the window that rattled, no matter how many novels I stuck between the panes. I rarely answered my phone in the hours between waking and stepping out of my door. Even when there was a lover in the picture, I preferred to have my mornings to myself. In fact, I had always liked the idea of living with someone in two separate, adjacent apartments, like Frida Kahlo and Diego Rivera, with the little bridge between their two houses.

When I first moved to the apartment, I could see the Twin Towers if I leaned out the window. Now I saw sky for most of the year, until the tree outside thickened with leaves. From the roof, where I wasn't allowed, I had a view that sparkled in the sun, sparkled in the dark, and glowed in the magic hours between. I loved the irony of Manhattan's famous skyline and its billions of tiny lights; it is a view best enjoyed from the outside.

My neighborhood in Williamsburg had none of the cobblestoned good looks of the West Village or even Brooklyn Heights. But there was a kind of stark beauty in defiant grass growing in sidewalk cracks, the contrast of flower boxes in warehouse windows, breathtaking murals on unclaimed walls. As spring eased itself into the city, I wandered, stopping every few hours for coffee and a chapter. Cafés overflowed anytime but early mornings, for there were few commuters in the neighborhood at that time. After noon, the self-employed, or unemployed, hipsters set up their laptops, soy milk lattes by their side, and proceeded to create ironic and subversive works of art, pausing every so often to brood.

While waiting for Per Se to reopen, I completed my schoolwork for the rest of the semester and spent whole days reading entire books. Often, stocked with a bag of my own snacks, I saw two or three movies in a row. Edamame worked well, but garlicky steamed dumplings elicited stares. Sometimes I picked an unfamiliar neighborhood to explore and spent a few hours shopping for chocolate-chip cookies and town houses I was a few million dollars short of buying. One day, after spending hours wandering the city without speaking to a single person and feeling a little invisible, I decided to make a conscious effort toward that very state. I dressed all in black and sat quietly on a bench on Bedford Avenue for a while, watching waves of people emerge from the subway and the occasional pigeon landing. Eventually a man asked if he could sit down, thereby rendering me visible again and relieving me from my little experiment so I could go back to my apartment and my post at the window. This is how I spent my days.

I told few people about my parents' divorce but spent not a few evenings drowning my sorrows with my vacationing coworkers. I didn't need this drama. I didn't need a family. And I certainly didn't ever need a man who was sure to leave me when I was least expecting it. When it came to men, I decided they were good for one thing. Any woman who thought otherwise was kidding herself and needed a wake-up call.

With a new resolve to live life as a single-but-fabulous woman, I went ahead and kept dating. What did it matter anyway? It wasn't like I was planning on getting married anytime soon. Or ever.

THE FIRST GENTLEMAN had been in and out of town during our training, working on a project for the restaurant about which he had been vague. We saw a few movies and had a few drinks and when he came to the end of his hotel stay, I did the hospitable thing and welcomed him into my home for a few days until he flew back to California. This was where it went wrong. When I think about that weekend, I picture an intersection. (I don't drive a car, but I ride in one often.) I envision the kind of intersection without a light, where drivers take turns and politely wave one another through. In the case of this gentleman and myself, we alternated between staring at each other, drumming the pads of our fingers on the steering wheel (something I notice drivers often do when waiting their turn), and accelerating into head-on collisions. When he finally left, I went over to my bed to groan and pity myself for a while and then saw that he had tucked a piece of notepaper under the frame of my mirror with a simple sketch of an optimistic-looking daisy. "Flowers are best left to themselves," it read. "Unsupervised, they flourish." I agreed. But reading the note made me lonely in that kind of way one is lonely in a city of eight million people, when an empty connection is worse than being alone. I have few fond memories of that weekend, but I kept that note on my mirror until I moved two years later.

I entered false start number two with a new coworker, knowing that this whole single-but-happy act was a sham. I still thought good relationships were improbable and marriage was a lie, but dating couldn't hurt. This was a serious crush, which involved a lot of eyelash-batting and real dates.

I even let him pick the restaurants. I was more used to dates that began with "I have this thing on Friday night" or "Do you want to share this cab?" The first time he kissed me, he paused a few inches from my lips to whisper, "May I?"

I began to say things to my friends like "I have high hopes for this one" and "He might be a keeper!" He was one of the French Laundry staff living in the rented apartments on Fifty-seventh Street and, like many newcomers, loathe to travel outside of Manhattan. We spent more time in his building, which I understood also housed a few captains, some cooks, and André and Leigh, though I rarely saw any of them.

And then, on my birthday, he ended up in the men's bathroom with a girlfriend of mine. I didn't know this until the next morning, after my leather jacket had been stolen at the club, after he had come home with me and consoled me, after I had made him breakfast in the morning and left him asleep in my bed to go, starry-eyed, to meet the friend. She said he started it, he said she followed him in and attacked, and I sent both of them packing, too hurt to sort out the truth. It just so happened that I had already planned a party for myself and invited twelve girlfriends. Diva in distress! Send up a smoke signal! They arrived, bearing the four things I love most in this world (besides a whole bunch of other things): cheese, bread, chocolate, and red wine. When I told my mother about it later, she observed that these were all known to cause migraines.

So with a few Band-Aids on the ego and a new resolve to be fabulous, I charged on into false start number three. The birth-day incident had stung, but I took the advice of the girls and got right out there again. One of the chefs at work had been bugging me to go out and, when he came through with a partic-ularly good reservation, I agreed. "I am now, officially, a food whore," I told a friend after I said I would go. He was perfectly sweet and even arrived with a box of chocolates. As painful as it was, I did seem to be getting the hang of this dating thing.

One never means to get so drunk and one never means to make extreme errors in judgment, but this one did. And when we awoke, I couldn't get out of my house fast enough.

"Is it a one-night stand if you have coffee the next morning?" he asked.

"Of course not," I cooed through clenched teeth and walked him to the subway.

I was hungover, embarrassed, and furious with myself. That was it. Just like Marilyn Monroe did at the end of *Some Like It Hot*, I would swear off love. Of course, as she professed the sentiment, she draped herself over a piano with her best come-hither pouts and her breasts spilling over a tiny cocktail dress. Furthermore, she ended up with a broke, womanizing saxophone player with a gambling habit. I might want to find another model for my despair.

THANKFULLY, I SOON had little time for despair. The restaurant was ready to reopen. The second opening took on a whole new tone. We were rested and ready to work and, after two months, truly happy to see one another. In the beginning, we had quite a few French Laundry staff to help us, but many of them had gone back to California to reopen the French Laundry. This time around, we would have no one to lean on, a fact that resulted in a deepened sense of camaraderie. The management had been busy, ordering the supplies proven needed during our first opening, organizing our workspaces, and creating more efficient storage. Someone, clearly, had bought a label maker.

Before the fire, we saw the kind of press for which most restaurants would kill. Numerous articles portrayed Chef Keller as the prodigal son, back with something to prove. Other pieces told the story of the Time Warner Center's glamorous restaurant collection. After the fire, Per Se stole the spotlight, as headlights documented the sheer extravagance of the restaurant, the five-thousand-square-foot kitchen, the pricey stove. Informed guests came in asking whether it was true that we had a special sixty-two-degree room for making and storing chocolates. Friends who knew nothing about food and restaurants quoted the reservation policy to me, as well as the price of the menus, and a few famous dishes.

The biggest difference between the second opening and the first was the pace. Unlike the initial weeks of training, we had only a few refresher sessions this time around. After we had raced through those, there was barely enough time for friends-and-family, let alone for the staff to dine again. Before we knew it, we were working service as if we had never closed.

Within days of our second opening, guests had posted reviews of their experiences on blogs and foodie Web sites. Comments on the food were, on the whole, complimentary. Impressions of the room were less so. Early critics found the browns and grays drab, the lines stark and sterile, the marble and glass cold. At best, they described the room as "cosmopolitan." The room was certainly not quaintly modeled after a farmhouse, as was the fashion in many of the "produce-driven" restaurants around the city; it did not have rococo scrolls and ornate flowers, the crushed velvet/bordello look, or the tarnished mirrors of a faux bistro. But to find fault with this would be to miss the point. The well-spaced tables, muted colors, and clean lines remained understated on purpose. To further the calming effect, the room was quiet (except for the occasional deafening fire alarm). Even the traffic in Columbus Circle swarmed in silence four stories below. Here, the vibrancy, humor, and artistry occurred on the plate and in the experience of dining.

It was one thing to critique the room, but when early reviews called the dining room staff somber, we were dismayed. This was exactly what we wanted to avoid. "Invisible" we could live with, but "ghostly" we would not. One could argue that good service is subjective. Some people find a waiter cold if she doesn't introduce herself, treat the host like her favorite uncle, and write "thank you!" on the check in bubble letters. Others prefer an unsmiling man with an accent, a master of the bow-and-retreat default move.

These two varieties of service, the "Comin' Right Up" variety and the "But of Course" variety, are only two in a broad spectrum of reserve. But I think everyone would agree that "funereal" should be avoided. This was not what Laura had in mind when she shaped the service style at the French Laundry. She designed it to be elegant yet relaxed to complement the luxury and the whimsy of the food. Laura herself exemplified this balance. I had found her intimidating until I realized that, like so many unreadable people, she was actually shy. Once she knew you, she greeted you like a friend and had this way of looking at you as if expecting something hilarious and slightly scandalous. Which, of course, inspired you to provide just that. It didn't surprise me that she had all but escaped the spotlight while orchestrating a world-famous dining room. Guests and press often walk into a restaurant and ask "Who does your flowers?" but they rarely walk in and ask "Who hires and trains your staff?" She managed, like the best in the service industry, to make it seem effortless and fade into the background.

There were two points to address if we were to honor Laura's philosophy. The first was the issue of tableside service, which occasionally required so many hands that a table of two might be completely obscured by somber servers. The Cappuccino of Forest Mushrooms, for example, called for one person to hold the soup terrine on a tray, one to hold mushroom biscotti, the mushroom foam, and the mushroom dusting powder (à la cinnamon) on a tray, and one to serve the soup. If a maître d' stepped in to help, he made four. If the sommelier happened to be around pouring wine, he became a fifth. The backserver pouring water and serving bread made six. Soon after this review, we streamlined tableside service and made a rule that, unless completely necessary, no more than two people should attend a table at any given time.

The second issue came down to not taking ourselves so damn seriously. It seemed that, in the months of learning how to walk and talk and correctly place a glass on a table, we had forgotten the point of good service. It was like a man learning to waltz, muttering "*One*, two, three, *one*, two, three" under his breath and staring at his feet. Only when he stopped thinking and started feeling—the beat, his partner's hand, the slight weight of her arm on his—would he begin to dance. True, we had been taught to place the wineglass to the right of the guest, directly above the knife. But only so as to be conveniently close to her right hand. If she moved it to the left, it behooved us to make room for it there and alert anyone else serving the table so no one moved it back. If a guest wanted ice in his vintage champagne, we should offer ice with the Corton-Charlemagne as well. If a runner noticed that the table seemed irritated when he spieled the first course, he should alert the other runners to make it brief on future courses. As I watched the seasoned French Laundry staff, I noticed how often they bent the rules they knew so well in order to accommodate the guest. In one such instance, one of the runners delivered a dish to a table, an element of which was nuage. When the guests looked at her with confusion, she leaned in and, with a conspiring roll of the eyes, whispered, "Foam."

There's a fine line between being a graceful server and being a pompous ass. Grace depends entirely on keeping the focus on the guest, not on the server or the act of serving. Take the removal of cloches, the hatlike pieces of china placed over certain dishes to keep them warm. When serving the Bichalots the Oysters and Pearls, for example, the runner carried a dish in each hand. He placed the first in front of Mrs. Bichalot and the second in front of Mr. Bichalot. Then he walked back over to Mrs. Bichalot to remove the cloche from her dish before returning to remove his. The runner's spiel, begun during or after the decloching, might go "This is Oysters and Pearls: Island Creek oysters and Iranian osetra caviar in a sabayon of pearl tapioca." Then he would NOT say "Enjoy," but smile and depart.

If there were more than two guests, two servers removed both sets of cloches in unison. A party of six required three servers, and so on. Sometimes, if a few sommeliers, managers, or backservers happened to be nearby, six of us might remove six cloches in unison. Depending on how we danced, it could be seamless and elegant, everyone moving together, every guest served at once. But if someone removed the cloche with a giant fanfare or studied precision, the effect was ruined. Now, what was meant to simply keep a dish warm became a pretense. It was a fine line and one we had to master if we were to make people comfortable. Depending on the table, that might mean making a joke while removing the cloches. I once served a man who got a kick out of taking his cloche off himself. When it was time to remove the next set of cloches, I stood behind him and said, "Now!" It may have been against the rules, but at least it wasn't funereal.

• A TIP •

There's no need to say that you are allergic when you don't like something. Not only are allergies very serious, but you have every right to your personal taste.

• four-star mistress •

---

tHE SECRET TO service is not servitude, but anticipating desire. This occurred to me in the plenty of time I had to eavesdrop, while marking tables and refilling water glasses. If I overheard something important—that the guests were getting full, that they had a babysitter at home, or that he preferred fruit desserts to chocolate—I reported it to the captain. The captain might then ask whether they still wanted the cheese course, box up some macaroons for the babysitter, or switch the guest's dessert without his having to ask. This had nothing to do with obeying the commands of the sort of demanding customer who snaps his fingers from across the room. Garçon! Miss! This was about the art of careful observation and the intimacy of knowing what someone wants before he does.

When we lost our first captain, soon after our second opening, I was given the opportunity to practice this art full-time. The captain in question was a wry but reserved Frenchman in his late forties who had worked in some of the finest restaurants in the city. He wore gray sweater cardigans and pleated khaki pants. One day, we were all huddled around large round tables in the windowless private dining room taking another one of our cippolini/cipolini/cipollini/cipolinni kind of tests when he stumbled in, wild-haired, decked out in a Hawaiian shirt and sunglasses, and drunk. Upon entering, he began a highly amusing monologue, asking questions in a painfully slow slur as the rest of us tried to remain focused on the test.

"I am having trouble with number eighteen. Can someone define 'sense of urgency'?" The phrase probably took a good twenty seconds to get out.

Managers rushed in. Ever calm, Laura locked eyes with the director of operations and silently ran her forefinger across her neck. He excused us immediately for an early lunch, and when we returned, we were down one captain.

Whenever possible, the company promoted from within, so it was from the pool of backservers that the next captain was to be selected. Since they were looking for presence and charm, I knew Patrick would be the first pick. But as it turned out, they also wanted a woman. I was surprised when the director of operations took me aside and told me that Patrick and I were both on the "fast track" to being captains and that our training would commence immediately.

It would be a relief to talk about something other than the bread, butter, and water selections. As a backserver, from the moment the first table entered my section to the time I had changed all the tablecloths at the end of the night, I moved nonstop. Pouring, marking, clearing, surviving the wrath of the captain who had barely survived the wrath of a chef or maître d' and needed someone to blame. It was an exhausting job, but at least the time went by quickly. Being a captain, on the other hand, would carry more responsibility, but it would also be a hell of a lot more fun. No longer would I feel like a marking machine. I could make real connections with the guests, get to know the chefs better, and become even more familiar with the food.

In terms of food and service, I had been pretty well prepared during our initial training. What I hadn't learned about my new duties then, I had figured out while working closely with the captains every night as a backserver. Knowing all of the other backservers as peers allowed for an even easier transition. I was aware of their strengths, weaknesses, and quirks and knew when to help them and when to ask them for help. The real trick would be mastering our medieval computer system and learning to withstand the whims of the chefs. When I made a mistake on the floor, I now reported to the expediting chef who stood at the pass. Jonathan Benno worked half of the shifts and, despite the persimmon business, we got along well most of the time. Corey Lee, feisty, Korean, and prone to biting sarcasm, worked the other half. It was clear from my first day as a captain that Corey did not like me in the slightest.

During my training, I trailed other captains, learning how to translate a guest's request into something the kitchen could do and not hate me for. For example, at Per Se, meat was cooked au point, which translates as "to the point of perfection." Every cut of meat had its own point of perfection. Tougher cuts like shoulders should be braised for hours, but venison or a wild game bird would be tough and liverlike if overcooked. If guests asked, we would tell them how the chef preferred to cook the dish, but the decision was ultimately theirs. Say Mr. Bichalot, for example, has ordered the nine-course chef's tasting menu, on which we are serving duck breast as the first meat course. He requests that his duck be cooked "to a crisp." When the captain goes to the kitchen to make the request, the chef will say that he is perfectly happy to cook the quack out of it, but we both know that it does the duck no justice. Might the guest like a braised pork shoulder? Mr. Bichalot loves the pork, the chef feels good about serving a dish he is proud of, and the captain has made no enemies.

I was quickly learning that, although the chef's tasting menu was set, almost any change could be made to accommodate the guest. One perfect example, of which I became the mistress, was what I called the chef's tasting menu for pregnant women. I think we can all agree that the first rule when dealing with pregnant women is never to ask unless absolutely sure. The salmon cornet usually gave it away because most pregnant American women are deathly afraid of anything raw. Immediately, we sent them a cornet made with tomato confit and eggplant caviar. Then they would be assured that the oysters were poached. We might discuss fish options depending on mercury levels, the extent to which they wanted their meat cooked, and whether the cheese (goat, cow, sheep, blue) was pasteurized. I also became comfortable with the chef's tasting menu for the kosher guest (substitute cauliflower panna cotta without oyster glaze for the Oysters and Pearls, substitute second fish for lobster, first meat minus the crepinette, second meat no dairy, substitute salad for cheese, sorbet, substitute no-dairy dessert) and the chef's tasting menu for those who have been dragged to dinner and really just want a steak (soup, salad, pasta, lobster, steak, cheese, sorbet, dessert).

In contrast to the high-maintenance adults, we often hosted serious diners under the age of twelve. For some of them, we offered a few fun courses on the simpler side. Chef Keller insisted on feeding small children for free. Often the kitchen sent out something they called the "short stack," a tiny tower of potato blini, quarter-sized at the bottom up to dime-sized at the top.

They looked like pancakes, but tasted like mashed potatoes. There were also adventuresome children who wanted to do the tasting menu—the kind of kids who like their shrimp with the heads on. The whole staff fell in love with these young guests. Meanwhile, across the dining room sat the middle-aged man who refused to eat his vegetables, the woman who claimed to be allergic to anything too fishy, the food-phobic woman who started hyperventilating when she looked at the menu, the anorexic who spat all her food into the napkin that she shoved in a backpack under the table, the macho man who laughed at the portion size and demanded a few more meat courses before cheese, or the woman who became teary at the thought of eating anything on her personal "cute list," an arbitrary list of mammals. Apparently lobsters aren't cute. Across the room, Junior has cleaned his plate of rabbit rillette and is looking forward to a little stinky cheese.

Customizing people's menus took skill and patience, but pairing wines for the picky guest—or any guest for that matter—I still found challenging. No matter how many seminars I attended, books I read, and wines I tasted, I retained only a fraction of the knowledge. At restaurant tastings, the other captains discussed winemakers and soil variation while I was still trying to figure out what region we were talking about. And when it comes to vintages, I am still convinced that a mind that can recall the difference between 1981 and 1982 Petrus is very similar to the mind that knows not only who won the World Series in 1981 and 1982, but also who pitched and in how many innings.

Because of my weakness in wine knowledge, André began to spend a lot of time in my section. We didn't have a wine pairing per se, but we often put together a program for guests who wanted to leave it up to us. In situations like these, we might use half bottles, and even beers, sakes, juices, teas, or spirits. I would have gone down flailing if it hadn't been for André. When a guest asked about different vintages or my recommendations for old Riesling from Alsace, André always just happened to be walking by. Soon I had the sense that he was watching my every move. And as time went by, I began to watch his.

"I have something for you," he whispered one day at the beginning of service and motioned for me to follow him off the floor. It was a wine key, exactly like the standard-issue key we all had. I looked down at it, unimpressed.

"Turn it over." A tiny white label stretched along the side with "Diva" in black lettering. The label told me he had, indeed, been watching me closely.

"So you don't lose it. It's left-handed, but don't advertise that—I had to buy a whole box of them."

"How did you know I was left-handed?"

"Chef," he answered, shaking his head as if disappointed in me. "I noticed. Plus, lefties seem to be my lot in life."

All potential lovers encounter a moment when the harbored crush becomes possible. In the movies, it is a look; in the theater, a subtle innuendo; in pastoral poetry, a stolen embrace followed by a blush of the pretty innocent's lily white breast. In reality, it's often chemically induced and somewhat predatory, though no less exciting when reciprocated. There are romantic exceptions, of course, as in the case of a chef I know who met a woman at a farmer's market and wrote his phone number on a squash. Or the sommelier who ordered an entire case of useless wine keys for the left-handed object of his affection. I can't be sure, but I have a feeling she blushed and smiled, like the shepherdesses and milkmaids, starlets and ingénues before her.

DESPITE MY LACK of wine knowledge, my fast track turned out to be about two weeks. The restaurant added more covers every night and had begun increasing the number of private dining events. This meant that we needed more captains on the floor. Furthermore, we expected the *New York Times* critic any day and wanted to make sure that the captains had manageably sized sections so as to have enough time for each guest. Patrick was ahead of me by a few days in our training and, even though he wasn't working a full station yet, already he was flourishing. He had always been personable, but his persona on the floor blossomed in the role of captain. Because of his small stature and boyish face, guests sometimes underestimated his wit and his knowledge of food and wine. By the end of the meal, they were asking people to "send the little fellow over" and clapping him on the shoulder on their way out. I also enjoyed my promotion when I began, but my experience was quite different from Patrick's.

For most of my first year working in fine dining, not only was I the only female captain at Per Se but, as far as I could tell, one of only two in the city's four-star restaurants. The image of the debonair Frenchman with a serviette draped over his arm still reigned, although a new wave of sleek-suited younger men was entering the field, no doubt spurred by a society with new *Gourmet* subscriptions and Food Network on TiVo.

The fact that I was aware of my gender in this world struck me as odd. It was as if I were some sort of inversion of an inversion. Wasn't hospitality or servitude in essence women's work? Apparently, when it involved six-figure salaries and health care, it wasn't. It took some time to understand where my own power lay and that I was at an advantage as a woman.

Although I wore a black suit and silk tie, I learned when to work the woman angle by exuding warmth and making guests feel at home. I learned that a domineering wife requires a much different approach than the ringleader of a group of lunching ladies. I interacted one way with the gentleman attempting to impress his date and another with the financial broker with his posse of drinking buddies. I was ally, authority, object, and confidante within a span of thirty seconds, but in every case assumed as much control over my tables as my male counterparts, no matter how subtle my hold.

As I had seen as a backserver, our greatest skill in the hospitality business is the ability to anticipate desire. If I did my job well, the guest would constantly wonder how I knew what he wanted before he did. When he asked to see the wine list again, it should be in my hand. When he motioned for the check, it was already on the table. If all went well, he was satiated not only by the food he was served, but by being given the attention he didn't know he craved. It was not uncommon for a previous guest to yield completely on his second visit. "You know what I like," he would say, handing back the menu and wine list. "I am in your hands."

Did putting guests at ease come more naturally to a woman? Or were we just used to using observation and empathy to our advantage? Did my male customers enjoy feeling like I was in charge or had they fashioned an angel-at-the-hearth role for me that they found comforting?

Fascinated by these dynamics, I began to observe gender politics on the floor of the dining room . . . wearing a boxy, unflattering suit, a shirt that buttoned to my chin, and a tie. I can think of only a few occasions for which a woman wearing a tie is appropriate: when meeting a female lover at the altar, when holding a cane and tap-dancing across a stage, or when protesting a gender-discriminatory uniform policy. In an age where women lead nations, corporations, and cultural, political, and religious movements, I find it hard to believe that a phallic noose is the best symbol of the power we could wield.

"How do you feel about female dominance?" I asked Truman, my backserver, one dinner as he set four water glasses and a coaster on a Christofle silver tray.

"I like it," he responded, affecting a pant, as he picked up the tray. "Corner!"

Before I had a chance to explain myself, Truman rounded the blind corner from our service station and strode toward table six, where one guest was nervously flipping through the thick, leather-bound wine list. Truman placed each Orrefors water glass just below and to the right of the Spiegelau wineglass, the other edge of which had been directly aligned with the outer edge of the Ercuis knife. Both of us, if asked, could give you a brief history of each company, its geographic location, and a few of their lines of product. Table six opted for sparkling water, which meant Truman would pour Tŷ Nant, a Welsh water with tiny, tight bubbles. A perfect food water. Had they requested still water, they would have chosen between the crisper Hildon, from Southwest England, or Wattwiller. The latter, specially imported for us from Alsace, I always described, with an almost undetectable smirk, as more "fullbodied." If guests laughed or rolled their eyes at this, I knew we would get along just fine.

As in all services, we were working in a two-"man" team, this night in VIP-heavy station two. This meant we would pour free champagne and offer to prepare a special menu. If the guests were foodies or press, they usually loved the attention. If they were celebrities with a nutritionist to see in the morning or CEOs with an early meeting, they would start to squirm after the soup, savory sorbet, caviar, fish, custard, and meat canapés, all of which come before the meal has really begun. Tonight, as we learned in the preservice meeting, Truman and I would be waiting on an influential socialite who was well known in the gossip columns (light on the canapés) and a British celebrity chef in town for a book signing (heavy on the organ meats).

As I quickly polished fingerprints off the sterling silver clasps of four menus, I regretted having thought aloud to Truman, of all people. Most of the other captains dreaded working with him because he was cocky and quick-tempered, but he and I got along well. It wasn't the easy, unspoken rhythm I had with some of the other backservers, particularly the women. I was constantly making room for Truman in a variety of ways, complimenting him on being able to run the station without me, letting him take over some of my captain's duties like readying glassware and taking drink orders while I served bread and poured water. If this didn't soothe him, all I had to do was ask about his daughter. They weren't living together these days, but he picked her up and took her to school every morning, no matter his hours the night before. Recently, we had been working on a new lunch menu for her second year of school. My days nannying had kept me current on trends in elementary school dining, but he clearly spent his fair share of time in the grocery aisles as well.

Maybe we tolerated each other because I wasn't particularly easy to work with either. I had a reputation of being merciless at times. After a particularly busy night working with me, one of the newer backservers nursed his wounds over a beer and complained that I had ridden him hard. After that, I tried to take it easy on Seabiscuit, as we subsequently named him. When he worked hard and fast, I called him Bisquick.

Back in station two, I had finished taking the order on table six when I noticed their water glasses had gotten low.

"Even in jail you get bread and water," I scolded Truman, since he enjoyed female dominance.

As Truman poured, the maître d' seated our socialite on table three. André had readied the champagne in the ice bucket, the chef fired two gougères in the kitchen, and I polished two more menus. I realized that I never explained my question to Truman and wondered whether he had forgotten about it when he barreled around the corner again.

"Think we will make it into Page Six tomorrow?" he asked, tossing the breadbasket noisily back onto the service station.

"We can always dream," I responded, gathering the menus. "Let the kitchen know they can send those gougères any day."

Truman was already halfway down the hall, but he paused and turned with a grin.

"Yes, mistress."

AFTER A FEW months as a captain, I congratulated my feminist self on breaking through the glass ceiling of fine dining. I was getting important tables, I had health care and dental, I had set up a new 401(k) account (now that I had figured out what it was), I was respected by my male peers and making inroads for the women working just beneath me. And, most important, I was making the same amount of money as the men. Or was I?

Our term for the stealthy act of slipping cash to someone, while both parties pretend to be exchanging simple pleasantries, was a "handshake" or a "palm." The rule at Per Se was that all handshakes had to be turned into the house so that all the cash could be equally divided among the staff. This caused a lot of grumbling among maître d's, sommeliers, and captains who felt they deserved the extra cash because they had been singled out for exemplary service.

As the resident restaurant leftie, I hopped right up on my soapbox to defend the rights of the common man. How could we have the arrogance to believe we could stand at a table for ten minutes discussing art or literature or wine or even politics (except during the Republican National Convention, when I decided that if I didn't have anything nice to say . . .) if it weren't for the backservers, runners, and bussers running their asses off to make sure the restaurant kept moving? And then it occurred to me that it was easy to preach since I was rarely tempted by cash myself.

It comes down to this: No matter how you frame it, when a man slips cash to a woman, it feels like it was just left on the bureau. How do you explain that to your date? I can just hear the voice of the jealous wife. "I see she made quite an impression on you."

As I was the only woman, I couldn't compare notes with peers, so I went to our only female maître d' and asked her opinion on the matter. At her last job, at a swank French bistro, the men walked out with $700 on some evenings when she was lucky to get $200. Her theory was that a man giving money to another man is a way for them to affirm their hierarchy. Although the captain, sommelier, or maître d' sets the tone of the meal, knows more than the guest does about wine, or seats him in the coveted corner table, once the guest slips him some cash, the guest is back on top.

The final piece of the puzzle is the kicker. While men palm other men out of discomfort with the master/slave dynamic, they are perfectly comfortable with a woman serving them. In fact, it is assumed that she enjoys it, that she is nurturing by nature, that she could never threaten the hierarchy. She will be lucky to get a thank-you, a good word put in to the boss, or even a pinch in the ass for her services.

Which begs the question of how women handle this situation. I have only once been palmed by a woman, and it was a most awkward exchange, involving a lot of fumbling and blushing. This is not what we women do. My greatest rewards from women have been kisses on the cheek, a whispered thank-you for helping them manage their mothers-in-law, and even an invitation to tea.

One day I had a table of five men and one woman, who was in charge, although she was clearly catering to the man sitting across from her. I circled the table on my initial approach, trying to figure out who was the host and who was the alpha (not always the same person). Finally, still stumped, I positioned myself to the right of the catered-to man and in direct eye contact with the woman. I offered the wine list. He took it. I explained the menu and suggested the chef's tasting menu, as I always do. Most of the party went with my suggestion, but the wooed man wanted the sweetbreads from the five-course menu.

"Could you show me to the ladies'?" the woman asked in her best woman-to-woman tone.

"Of course," I responded, reluctant to leave the men alone with the menus. If they started tinkering with the chef's tasting and ordering only the biggest and cheapest California Cabernets, I would hold her responsible.

"Here's the deal," she said when we were out of earshot, speaking in bullet points. "We will have the tasting menu. We will do a wine pairing for one-fifty a head. We will add an additional foie gras course. We need this client. Make us look good."

I went back to the table with her credit card in my pocket and gathered the menus from the men, whose attention had wandered from food to the usual one-upsmanship. I made sure the guest of honor had his sweetbreads, poured his wine first, batted my eyelashes until I was dizzy, and broke the company rule by touching his arm and shoulder whenever the opportunity arose. Each time I looked at the host, she winked at me. So far, so good.

I had to respect this woman. If we had not had that talk, the dynamic would have been different between us. She would have had to deal with me as a distraction and a threat to her authority, not as a weapon for her own cause.

"Perfect!" she whispered triumphantly when the meal was over, squeezing my arm. She allowed the men to let her go first and as I thanked the group, the client paused to shake my hand. And I felt it, the unmistakable wad pressing itself into my palm.

"Thank you."

"A pleasure, sir," I responded, slipping my hand into my pocket as I had seen it done so many times and glancing quickly around to see who might have witnessed it. I realized that all three of us knew what was going on; I had made her look good, and I had been a kind of ally for him. But was the cash his way of acknowledging the dance we had all done? Or did he feel unarmed without his credit card and ability to choose what he would eat? I pondered this as I walked up to the host stand to add my money to the cash tips we would divvy up at the end of the night. I was pretty sure that no one had seen the hand-shake, but the truth was, it wasn't about the money.

• A TIP •

Always call if you will not be showing up for a reservation. Making backup reservations and not showing up is like making multiple prom dates and then letting them wait all night in their living rooms, watching the clock in heels and hose and sagging up-dos.

• being frank •

Rule #36: Staff may attend wine industry events at the restaurant with approval from the wine director or head sommelier.

EVEN AFTER MY three disastrous affairs, not to mention three waves of feminism, my life in the summer of 2004 was defined by two men. The first was trouble, the second was torture. Because I had briefly been in charge of ordering wine at my first restaurant in Brooklyn, which now seemed completely absurd, I was on a few e-mail lists for wine distributors. I usually just deleted them, but one caught my eye: a biodynamic tasting at the Metropolitan Pavilion. Even though it was not being held at the restaurant, I decided to run this one by the wine department, and André in particular.

It's not like I'm asking him out on a date, I told myself; it's an industry event.

"Of course you should go," André assured me. "In fact, I might join you."

When I arrived at the tasting a few days later, he was waiting next to a table of empty glasses.

"Shall we?" he asked, taking one for each of us. Though he had only lived in the city for a few months, André ran into someone he knew every few steps. He introduced me by name only, leaving our relationship open to interpretation. Between acquaintances, we paired the wines we tasted to recent menu items, stopping every so often for a piece of cheese or bunch of grapes.

If the biodynamic wine tasting did not begin as a date, it felt like one by the end. Afterward, loosened by the wine and accustomed to each other's pace, we walked together toward the subway. Then, with a subtle nod of his head in the direction of the pub across the street, he led the way. Circumstance spared us from the classic awkwardness of a first date. Not only had we achieved an ease with each other in the dining room, but my curiosity inspired an immediate inquisition. Since he had first introduced himself during training, I had wanted the whole story of how he went from slinging burgers in San Antonio to shaving truffles in New York.

"Does your family drink wine?" I asked him.

"Does white Zinfandel count?"

His cousin worked in restaurants, but that was about it for food and wine interest in André's family. His mother and his stepfather were both in the military and they had moved frequently, all around the country, to Germany, and finally to Texas.

"So how did you learn about wine?"

"From reading," he said. "And from other wine lists. I used to call restaurants and ask for a copy of their list. Then I would spread them all out on the floor and see which bottles they all had. Those were the ones I wanted to try."

I wasn't paying attention. I was silently narrating the potential downfalls of our potential love affair, besides his involvement with someone else. Military? Uh-oh, his mother would hate my politics and forbid him to see me. He played basketball in high school? Uh-oh, I could not date someone who watches the game when there is brunch to be had. Moved a lot as a child? Uh-oh, he's well traveled but potentially unstable. Self-taught? Uh-oh, possible workaholic. Eventually, the conversation came back to the restaurant and the topic on everyone's mind: the arrival of the *New York Times* reviewer. It was only a matter of time, we mused. André and I mused together frequently now, standing side-by-side so we could watch our tables as we whispered.

When I looked across my pint at André and listened to him segue from Burgundy to basketball to restaurant critics, I had one thought: Uh-oh. I refused to believe in The One, but this was certainly A One. He was also not a Suitable One, given the fact that he was in management and living with my coworker. When we left the bar and stepped back into the afternoons we had planned for ourselves, I envisioned a train leaving a station. The wheels had only barely budged, but if they gathered any more speed, there would be no stopping them. Eyes on the prize, I told myself: four stars.

THE SECOND MAN in my life was Frank Bruni, the new critic from the *New York Times*. In a rare moment of generosity, competing restaurants shared old pictures of the critic that were then posted behind host stands around the city with the caption "Have you seen this man?" God help the host who seated him at a less-than-desirable table by the door, the kitchen, or a busy service station.

In New York, a city that considers itself to be the center of the culinary—if not the whole—universe, the only restaurant review that means anything at all is that of the *New York Times*. In Paris, there are at least three sources that determine the fate of hotels and restaurants, all of which are rated by an anonymous group of reviewers who visit multiple times over the course of a year. *Le Guide Michelin* rates on a scale of three stars, *Mobil Travel Guide* rates with five, and *Relais et Château* simply adds the chosen restaurant to its exclusive list.

Like receiving a star from the *New York Times*, gaining a Michelin star means a dramatic increase in business and respect from one's peers, while losing one can be a serious blow to the heart and the cash register. In February 2003, amid rumors that his popular Côte d'Or restaurant in Burgundy would be demoted from the highest rating of three stars to two, Bernard Loiseau committed suicide, leaving the restaurant in the hands of his widow and three small children. This tragedy awoke the world to the pressure under which these reviewing systems put chefs and restaurant owners. The *Michelin Guide* came out with its first American edition in the fall of 2005, *Relais et Château* already ranked American establishments, and outside of New York, *Mobil Travel Guide* stars are quite a respected rating system. But within New York, it is still the *Times* that has the say.

André and I discussed the arbitrary star system one night after work. After the biodynamic wine tasting, we began to meet at the Coliseum, the bar where all of our coworkers convened. Soon we were sneaking off on our own. Some illicit lovers frequent cheap motels; we frequented cheap dive bars where we were sure to know no one. On one such occasion, we tackled the star system and decided to come up with a stars-for-dummies explanation for our friends and family who had no idea what all this excitement was about. I suggested that we liken the star system to sports, which people seemed to understand and enjoy. André helped me with the details. The four-star restaurants would be the pros; all respectable foodie fans keep up on new developments. Three stars would be college teams; well known but without the glitz of the pros. Two stars are local teams—maybe from our home state or small college; these are our go-to restaurants, places with good food, a casual vibe, a place where everybody knows your name. One stars and no stars are the high school teams; at best they have heart, at worst we check the clock every few minutes to see when it will be over.

Beginning on June 1, the eyes of New York's foodie fans were on Frank Bruni and the pros. Would Mr. Bruni, eager to prove himself stringent but fair, demote any of the four-star restaurants? Five restaurants held such distinction in the city, and all but one were French: Jean-Georges, Le Bernardin, Daniel, Alain Ducasse at the Essex House, and Bouley. And even though David Bouley was American, his dishes and techniques were French.

Unlike William Grimes, Bruni's predecessor, whose preferences and eccentricities were common knowledge, Frank Bruni was a mystery. We knew only that he had been stationed as a political reporter in Italy for the past few years and had written a book about George Bush. Would he like to be coddled or left alone? Did he prefer an underemployed actress with a good heart as his waiter or a stodgy Frenchman with a serviette draped over his immobile arm? Window table or something overlooking the dining room? California Chardonnay or white Burgundy?

Between the retirement of William Grimes and Mr. Bruni's first review, Amanda Hesser had acted as the *Times*'s temporary critic. She later came to Per Se, presumably not writing a review herself, but one could never be sure. We were almost positive it was her, but it was her husband, the famously reluctant "Mr. Latte," who gave her away. I had read her book about their courtship, *Cooking for Mr. Latte*, and she had described his pained look perfectly. Former *New York* magazine reviewer Gael Greene and former *Times* reviewers Mimi Sheraton and Ruth Reichl dined at Per Se as well. During each of their tenures, they had different styles but were all known for taking great precautions to disguise themselves. Would Mr. Bruni attempt the same? William Grimes had come to my last restaurant without a disguise. He tasted almost everything on the menu under the scrutinizing eye of hidden restaurant cameras linked to a wall of screens in the kitchen. Every move was analyzed by the managers and chefs with eyes glued to the screens as well as by one of the owners, who peered out from behind a newspaper from across the room where he was pretending to dine.

To be fair, the job of a critic is grueling and heavily scrutinized. Few readers would pretend to be more qualified than experts reviewing, say, Supreme Court verdicts or new discoveries in astrophysics, but in terms of food, they all consider themselves experts. But it is one thing to dine out a few times a week; eating out seven to ten times a week is another. When the average diner encounters lukewarm spaghetti and rude service, he makes a mental note never to return. When a critic experiences such trauma, he not only returns, but suffers through the entire menu over multiple visits and forces his friends to suffer along with him. Imagine the invitation: "Would you like to have dinner with me at the worst restaurant I've been to all year? I'll pay. . . ."

Still, at Per Se in the summer of 2004, empathy for the misunderstood and overworked critic was the last thing on our minds. Every day in our preservice briefing, we heard a variation of the same terror-inducing speech: Every table should be treated as a critic. Of course, for a while there it really felt as if there was a critic at every table. But we soon began to joke with one another. "Bruni's in your section tonight!" "No way, I saw him on table seven."

AND THEN, SUDDENLY, he *was* on table seven. We had expected him at any moment, and still he managed to show up when we were least expecting it. He was slightly thinner than his picture suggested, but he had the same brown hair parted conservatively to one side, the same brown eyes. He was wearing a plain suit. In short, he had nailed the everyman look. Unfortunately, we spotted him after Patrick had taken the order—on his first official day as captain. This was not a recipe for success in the eyes of management. However, since Patrick had already taken the order, there was no way to move a more experienced captain to that section without arousing suspicion, so he finished out the table. Any eyes not on Mr. Bruni were on Patrick.

Managers hovered in the shadows and hid behind the flower arrangements; maître d's paced the dining room trying to seem busy. Since we had nothing to go on, it was hard to know whether to read Mr. Bruni's reserve as his personality or whether we should assume that he was having a miserable time. Or maybe he was also a little nervous; after all, this would be one of his first big reviews.

Despite the stress, Patrick was magnificent. He even cracked one of the sarcastic jokes he had become famous for at the restaurant. Earlier in the meal, someone at the table was served the rabbit rillette and it didn't go over well. Besides mullet and the bizarre sorbets our pastry department concocted, the rillette was one of those dishes that people felt strongly about. Some people requested it as soon as they sat down, others found it dry, stringy, or salty. Mr. Bruni's table fell into the latter camp, causing much anxiety throughout the kitchen. When Patrick arrived four courses later to serve dessert, the mood was still a little stiff. Patrick's role in this course was to pour warm chocolate over a generous scoop of orange-scented vanilla ice cream. After a few seconds the chocolate would harden into a shell, much like a creamsicle, for which the dish was named. In the silence that accompanied his practiced drizzle, Patrick commented that perhaps he should have done this to the rabbit. There was a pause, the table erupted into hearty laughter, and a collective sigh rang throughout the restaurant. One visit down, at least two more to go.

It seemed everyone had a different theory about when Frank Bruni would come back. He would come on a Sunday, since that is often the chef's night off. He would visit twice, back-to-back. He would wait a few weeks between and see if we improved. He would have to come for lunch. He wouldn't bother with lunch. He was planning to get the review done as soon as possible. He would try to delay until the fall when readers came back from vacation. I have to believe that such speculation occurred on the floor as well as off.

All restaurants have ways of knowing when a critic is coming. There is the tip-off—from any number of sources in the know. There is the sighting—sometimes by the staff, sometimes by a fellow diner who happens to be in the business. In fact, managers and maître d's are even known to show up at one another's restaurants when a critic has been spotted so as to know whom to look for in the future. Often, a restaurant has a record of phone numbers and, when suspicious, can check to see if a certain number has been used before.

If someone is asking a lot of questions, that is always a sign. Adam Platt, of *New York* magazine, was notorious for this and actually made one of our best runners cry when he asked not what was in the dish (which she knew by heart), nor the source of the ingredients (the purveyors of which she knew by name and possibly by face), nor where the china was from (which she could point out on a map). According to the runner, he asked what our escargot ate.

Another fairly unpopular critic arrived for a ten o'clock reservation having already had dinner. He and his guests took one bite of each dish, including the salmon cornets, and pushed the plates away. After about two courses, we not only knew who he was, but knew where we'd like to tell him to go.

We did have some new information: Mr. Bruni had flown out to California and dined at the French Laundry. Laura recognized him while he and his guest had champagne in the garden before being seated. Chef Keller, who still spent most of his time in California, offered to prepare a special menu, and he accepted. We had expected Mr. Bruni to visit the French Laundry for research purposes, but would we suffer for it? Could we even hope to compete with Thomas Keller in the kitchen, a team of ten-years'-seasoned staff, and a garden filled with hummingbirds and blooming summer flowers? We began to strategize for the next visit.

BY ONE MEANS or another, we tentatively expected Mr. Bruni the next time he came. There was some debate about who should wait on him. Should it be someone who had experience from the French Laundry, or someone at Per Se? The diva inside of me desperately wanted the table. I loved those high stakes, the sense of performance, the feeling that what I did really mattered. A larger part of me got cold sweats whenever I thought about it. Finally, it was decided that Michael, who had spent time at both restaurants and had waited on Mr. Bruni in California, would take the table. When I arrived at work that day, the director of operations called me into the small private room at the end of the main dining room. Through the big glass window, I saw the other captains eyeing us as they set up their tables.

"I am going to cut to the chase," he began. "We want you to backserve for Michael on the Bruni table tonight."

My heart sank. This was the worst of both worlds—all the tension and none of the fun. Not only did I hate backserving, I had not worked the position in a while and was terribly out of practice. Immediately a collage of potential mishaps flashed in my mind, dumping the entire breadbasket on the carpet, pouring water all over the table, marking the wrong silverware, or just getting behind and lost. Having accomplished all of these quite recently, my fears were far from irrational.

"I don't know . . . I am really out of shape for this. Are you sure you don't want Mona to do it?" I considered my friend Mona to be the best backserver, much more polished than I would be.

After a moment, I took a deep breath and agreed. The rationale for my being the backserver was that I would observe Mr. Bruni and get to know his style and particularities before I took the table the next time. When that happened, I would be welcome to choose whomever I wanted as my backserver. Mona went over the markings for the most recent canapés, reminding me which needed an oyster fork or a chilled bouillon spoon, which meats required serrated knives, the names of all the breads—all things I had stopped paying close attention to. I reviewed the frenching technique that I had practiced for hours when I first took the job, holding two spoons together like tongs and carefully stacking thin pieces of the walnut bread we would serve with the cheese course onto a bread plate.

Mr. Bruni did come that evening. He sat with another food writer we also recognized and two other friends. He showed up later than his guests in tinted, plum-colored oversized glasses straight out of the late 1970s. He hadn't shaved in at least a week and looked a little like a Williamsburg hipster, minus the $200 jeans and trucker hat. We were amused but not fooled. I liked that this was the disguise he had chosen and that he took off the glasses after a few minutes when it was clear that everyone knew who he was.

They were right; marking every course, pouring water, and clearing plates gave me a good sense of Mr. Bruni's personality. Unlike some reviewers, who seem to start each meal with the attitude that they should be convinced to have a good time, Mr. Bruni came to the table as if ready to have a good time and inviting us to make it happen. Much to the relief of J.B., the chef de cuisine, he agreed to an extended menu just as he had done at the French Laundry. This way, if he were comparing the two restaurants, at least it would be a fair comparison—that is, if I didn't dump a bowl of soup in his lap. With the hopes of doing such a menu, J.B. had prepared a chart beforehand. It was divided into four columns for the four guests, each row having different preparations of each course. They would begin with four chilled soups (four chilled bouillon spoons), followed by four preparations of caviar (four mother-of-pearl spoons, an oyster fork for the pickled oyster, and an iced teaspoon with a long, thin handle to scoop our apple granita), and so on. They must have had twenty or so courses and close to eighty different dishes.

I have heard reviewers talk about how they make notes while at a restaurant. Some have a hidden microphone, others a hidden pad. I remember one saying that he divided the responsibility of remembering certain courses among his guests. Mr. Bruni had yet to figure out how to navigate this and got up between almost every course, clearly going to write it all down in the bathroom. This was a nightmare for the kitchen, because we never delivered food to a table when one person was up. It was also imperative that the food be perfect, meaning that many times they would have to start from scratch. The night of his second visit, eager to make up for the rabbit rillette incident, the kitchen prepared a degustation of rabbit, featuring a tiny rack with three toothpick-sized bones and a kidney the diameter of a dime. Corey, the sous chef, was working the meat station that night and was just placing a single leaf of chervil between the ribs when a runner came into the kitchen.

"Table three is up!"

Everyone swore and threw up their hands before quieting down and waiting in anxious silence, their eyes shifting from the clock on the wall to the plate of rabbit that was growing colder by the minute. Minutes passed as Mr. Bruni madly scribbled away in his stall.

"Replate," J.B. finally called, pushing four perfect plates in the direction of the dish station with a growl of frustration.

"Table three is back!" exclaimed the panting runner who had been assigned to be the eyes in the dining room.

"Perfect," J.B. responded with forced calm, knowing that it would be minutes before he could get another rabbit out. This happened not a few times over the course of the evening. And then everyone crossed their fingers, hoping another guest wouldn't find it an optimal time to go make a call, have a smoke, or write a novella in the bathroom.

By the time table three reached the end of their meal, they were the only ones left in the dining room. Though I had spilled nothing and managed to keep their bread plates and water glasses full, I hardly felt victorious. Mr. Bruni would be back. And next time, I would be required to speak.

"Second best meal of his life," Michael called out with his usual bravado as he brought the last dessert plates past the anxious pastry department into the dish room.

"Second only to his last meal at Per Se," Corey retorted, knowing perfectly well that Michael had meant the French Laundry.

I observed this exchange with jealousy. Corey and I never had such a lighthearted conversation. In fact, every time we tried to speak to each other it seemed to go awry within seconds. I showed up in the kitchen at the wrong times, asked too many questions during service, and gave too many details about guests' requests. But the more sarcastic and short he was with me, the harder I tried to find my way to his good side, if there was one. And the harder I tried, the more I got under his skin. It was Mr. Wilson meets Pollyanna, and it wasn't pretty. One day after service, hoping to discover the after-hours, softer side of Corey, I poked my head into his office to say good night. He didn't look up.

"Corey, why do you hate me so much?"

"I don't hate you," he said with disdain, still not looking up.

"Because I have never had such a hard time communicating with anyone in my life," I said. Corey put down his pen and swiveled around in his chair.

"Are you one of those people who has to have everyone like you all the time?"

"Umm, I guess. . . ." I wasn't sure there was a right answer to this question.

"Because I am not one of those people." He swiveled back in his chair and picked up his pen again.

"Clearly," I said to his back and walked down the hall toward the exit. As always I was torn between being stung by his comment and amused that someone could be so blunt. I resolved, as I always did after one of our awkward exchanges, not to let him get to me. But I knew that I would still try to win his favor.

André, Frank, and now Corey.

• A TIP •

In more formal restaurants, let someone know when you are getting up to smoke or to make a phone call. Even better, let them know one course ahead, so the chef doesn't start your dish until you return.

• no bones about it •

---

aREN'T RESTAURANTS PRETTY much about cocaine and sex?" my cousin interrupted. I don't recall the topic on which I was pontificating, but it was probably something fascinating like the varied structure of salt crystals or why the women's uniform shirts had no collar stays. I answered that while there were surely plenty of restaurants out there for which this might be true, my colleagues and I preferred to hold our own wine tastings for recreation. At this point, he shot me a look I hadn't seen since seventh grade.

He was on to something, though. The job lends itself to late nights and revelry. Some abuse whiskey; others turn to bacon cheeseburgers. At the end of a tough shift, a waiter has been "on" for at least eight hours, sprinting around the dining room, catering to the whims of the guests and the chef, with little to no time for a water break or trip to the restroom. He is exhausted, starving, irritable, and wide awake. Lucky for him, all of his coworkers suffer as well, so they take their cash (or the promise of cash) and go out. Per Se was no exception.

Our restaurant fostered a sense of camaraderie in a number of ways besides sharing the same nickname of "chef." Initially, we bonded during training. Once we opened, we worked in teams each night, meaning that we not only knew our colleagues well, we depended on them. Most important, we all had "family meal" together every night, just like President Bush recommended to all families so their children would have good values and grow up to be gun-toting, pro-life, pro-death, gas-guzzling, warmongering, monolingual, homophobic, wiretapped, Bible-thumping, genetically engineered, stem cell–harboring, abstinent creationists. Oops, I think I just lost all of my red state readers. To make up for it, I'll let you lose my ballot. Per Se family meal didn't have this exact effect, but we did get to know one another better.

Family meal, called staff meal in some restaurants, is a reliably unreliable source of free food. It is common knowledge in most restaurants that when fish is past its prime, when the baker burned the bread, when the entremets boiled instead of parboiled the risotto, it goes to family meal. If there is duck breast on the menu, you can bet there will be duck legs for family meal. But no matter how much everyone complains and threatens to bring their own food the next day, they pile their plastic plates high.

At Per Se, each station in the kitchen took responsibility for one family meal dish. Garde manger made the salad, the fish station made the fish, meat cooked meat, and so on. Occasionally, the kitchen pulled out the stops and created some sort of culinary extravaganza, like the Mexican-themed family meal where someone made a watermelon salsa that put the tomato to shame. I recall Indian food one day, complete with a huge vat of lassi for us to ladle into plastic deli containers. A sous chef with a gift for southern cuisine once made fried chicken, pulled pork, and cornbread so good, the family meal line actually applauded. Every week we had sandwich day, usually on Friday, and pizza day, usually on Saturday. Other than that, for better or for worse, the kitchen surprised us.

Family meal hit the pass at 4:20 on the dot and front-of-the-house staff, who had already ironed the tablecloths, decrumbed the chairs, and polished the water pitchers, made a plate for each of the cooks who were still frantically finishing their mise en place for the night's service. Although in the following hours, the cooks would snack on the ends of the lamb saddle and taste-test sauces as they went, front-of-the-house staff would not eat again for at least eight hours. Furthermore, depending on how late she was out the night before, a waiter may have downed a cup of coffee or a bagel before she stumbled into work, but family meal would most likely be her first real meal of the day. When the shift ended, anywhere from midnight to 2:00 A.M., she needed to sit down, she needed a beer, and she needed accessible protein.

"How do you stay thin eating food like this?" Guests used to ask, licking the caviar from their mother-of-pearl spoons. How they thought the restaurant would stay in business feeding 150 employees foie gras and Scottish langoustines was beyond me.

If it weren't such an obvious gift horse, I might have asked why they chose 4:20 P.M. as Per Se mealtime. Not only was it odd not to have rounded it to 4:15 or 4:30, but in some circles, 4:20 has a special significance. In Burlington, Vermont, where I went to high school, "420" was code for marijuana. "420, dude" could mean anything from "Would you like to join me in the woods behind the school?" to "I just got back from the woods behind the school—do my eyes look red?" Needless to say, there were mumbled jokes in the family meal line and in the breezeway where we ate dinner, perched on wooden stools, but those of us in the know chose to keep this little fact to ourselves. When it came to buying by the ounce, I suspect that most of us would have sprung for caviar before weed.

Save for two Muslim coffee servers and a few perpetually harassed vegetarians on the staff, most of us ate everything, the stranger the better. As we set up the dining room before family meal, the most common conversation was where we ate on our last day off or where we should go on our next. We shared tips on where to get the best tripe and cockscombs, commiserated about picky spouses, and sometimes argued heatedly. One day, while reporting about Landmarc, a new late-night place with a remarkably inexpensive wine list, one of the backservers mentioned the bone marrow dish.

"There is no way it could be better than Blue Ribbon," Patrick countered.

"I am afraid it might be." Brows furrowed, buffing rags paused midpolish, and a hush fell over the dining room. Patrick's face flushed as he tried to respond.

"Please tell me how that is possible," he finally said with forced calm.

From here a serious argument began. It even traveled to the kitchen, where cooks chimed in with technical critiques about the importance of the acid in the marmalade and how the bone is cut. Clearly, we needed to settle this and there was only one way: a bone marrow tasting.

When management posted the next week's schedule, Patrick and I were excited to see that he had Wednesday, my school day, off. I also enlisted Gabriel, one of the maître d's, and tried, to no avail, to convince Corey.

"Have you tried the bone marrow at Per Se restaurant?" he asked after lying about having to work.

"No, I must have missed it at family meal," I responded sarcastically, realizing too late that I had just set myself up for a rocky night.

Patrick and Gabriel invited their neglected spouses. Patrick's girlfriend, Mandy, reluctantly agreed to come, but Gabriel's fiancée deemed it gross and set a curfew. André was working, but even if he hadn't been, we tried to avoid social activities with people from Per Se.

After unscientifically polling our coworkers, we determined that there were three places in the running. We would begin at Landmarc, the aforementioned newcomer, because their wine list was outstanding and, more important, cheap, and we could drink there while waiting to convene. From there, we would head to Blue Ribbon, and end up at Crispo, an Italian place on Fourteenth Street, whose marrow I had suggested and secretly hoped would triumph.

AFTER CLASS ON Wednesday, I found Gabriel, Patrick, and Mandy waiting for me at the bar. Behind them, an open hearth glowed behind a row of charred and sizzling hanger steaks. Landmarc has the signature look of its Tribeca neighborhood: lofty ceilings, exposed brick, and a sort of industrial elegance. In the summer months, they set three or four small tables out front so diners could enjoy the exhaust fumes of West Broadway and a view of the sports bar across the street that throbbed with stale rock and roll. The crew was well into a few cocktails and had run into two sommelier friends from other restaurants who appeared to be intrigued by our quest.

"Let us know when the tripe tasting happens," they called to us as we relocated to a table.

We promised the host that she would have the table back in less than an hour. We decided on two orders of marrow, fries, and the foie gras dish, which none of us had yet tasted. Fat, fat, and more fat. I suggested that to be fair, we should drink the same wine at each place, but Patrick disagreed, arguing that the accompaniments to the dish should determine our wine selection. He ordered premier cru Chassagne Montrachet and I decided to leave control grouping to more serious scientists.

After we placed our order with the perplexed waitress, we set up the criteria by which we would judge. First and foremost were the bones themselves. The marrow needed to be in good condition, easily accessible, and well-seasoned. Good condition meant that it had the consistency of underdone Jell-O and would melt in the mouth without much encouragement like any fat, from butter to foie gras. We decreed that the bread, marmalade, and other chosen accompaniments should complement the dish, but were to be assessed individually.

The order came with three bones, each about three inches high. They were cut so that the marrow was accessible from the top, and were served with a small wooden fork with which to scoop it out. We assembled our first bites in silence, spreading the translucent marrow on the bread and topping it with the marmalade, which was a tangy onion and port concoction. Coarse salt, to be sprinkled either on the marrow or atop the marmalade, arrived in a cast-iron skillet, small enough to fit in the palm of your hand. A nice touch.

"Okay, I have something to say," said Gabriel as he adjusted his wire-rimmed glasses authoritatively and cleared his throat. He had not, until this point, been taking this whole experience as seriously as some of us, but this seemed about to change. "This bread is killing my marrow."

Gabriel's delivery of this assessment reminded me of a

news briefing. In fact, everything about Gabriel gave the impression that he had a very important message to deliver. He did not simply walk; he strode with his head high and his back as straight as the part of his hair. During the preshift meeting, when something either amused or angered him, his pale skin flushed slightly, as if it had just been vigorously scrubbed.

He was right, as usual. The bread was overcharred, lending a burned flavor to the easily overpowered flavor of the marrow. This is not to say that we didn't finish all six bones, the foie gras, and a whole basket of fries (mentally noting to ask for them extra crispy next time).

Our hour was almost up when we poured out the rest of the wine and then hurried outside to hail a cab. Within minutes, we climbed out of the cab into Spring Street. Compared to Tribeca, with its wide streets lined with converted factories and warehouses, the Village feels like an old-world dollhouse. The streets are narrow, the buildings small, and each trendy boutique seems flanked by yet another café.

The word cozy is overused in New York—usually for painfully small apartments—but whenever I hear it, I imagine Blue Ribbon. The floors are slanted and creaky and the tables so close, that when you squeeze a lemon wedge over your fried calamari, you are just as likely to hit your neighbor as you are your date. Tiered stands of chilled shrimp, oysters, cockles, and the odd lobster claws dangling off an edge, towered over many of the parties. We convinced the host to give us the one empty table that was being held for another party.

"We'll be out of here in no time," Patrick assured the waiter who appeared after we had been seated. He ordered his usual selection, Calera Pinot Noir, which he believed did justice to the oxtail marmalade. He had been hyping this marmalade for the duration of the cab ride. A "manly" marmalade, he proclaimed. I told him not to prejudice the jury.

"Let the record show that it is 8:40 and we are sitting in Blue Ribbon," Patrick proclaimed with mock gravity after he had ordered the wine.

For many restaurant workers, Blue Ribbon serves as a second home. It is always busy, the food is consistently fine, and they serve until four in the morning. I had been there many times, with André and with other friends from Per Se, but could not recall ever having set foot in the West Village hangout before midnight. We unfurled our napkins and tore into the warm loaf of bread that sat, round and dusted with flour, on a board in the center of the table. All of us had the menu memorized, but tonight there was no need to choose; we were there for one thing and one thing alone.

I often have a hard time admitting to being wrong, but in this case, it was clear. There would be no way to improve upon the perfection that is Blue Ribbon's bone marrow. First of all, the bones themselves are cut on both ends, meaning that, as Gabriel demonstrated with practiced ease, one could slide the little wooden fork around the marrow, loosen it, and simply lift the bone away. Left on the plate is a perfect cylinder of gently wobbling marrow waiting to be spread generously onto the thick, sweet, golden brown triangles of fresh brioche. And I would argue that the luxuriously rich oxtail marmalade, with its brunoise of carrot and onion, is not only manly, but the truly memorable part of the dish.

We were sluggish and sated as we labored toward the door.

"How were the bones?" our waiter asked. I loved him for that question alone.

Mandy, who until this point had been a cheerful companion, swore she could not stand another ounce of fat. "Can we order at least one thing green?" she begged as we all slid low in the back of the cab, patting our bellies apologetically.

"Yes, but we must power on!" I said in an effort to rally the troops. "Crispo is the dark horse." Patrick grumbled and seemed to revive a little at the challenge. Gabriel looked at his watch.

In truth, I knew the verdict already and wasn't surprised when the marrow at Crispo not only lagged in comparison to Blue Ribbon, but came in a distant third to Landmarc. The bones, although cut crossways and quite accessible, were topped with a sort of breadcrumb concoction that tasted bizarrely fishy, as if they were soaked in sardine fat. "Which would be fine if that was supposed to be part of the dish," said Mandy, who was happily munching on a prosciutto and apple salad from which she had carefully removed all the prosciutto. "But I get the feeling that it was inadvertent."

At this point, Gabriel's phone rang and he headed home obediently to his fiancée, who would have little sympathy for his aching belly. That left Mandy, Patrick, and me at our table in the courtyard with a terrible bottle of Rosso de Montalcino, a heap of prosciutto, and a barely touched mass of marrow before us.

"You're on your own for that tripe tasting," Patrick informed me.

"BRUNI'S ON TABLE six!" Patrick proclaimed cheerfully one evening soon after our tasting, with the usual twinkle in his eye and wry smile. He had already done his tour of Bruni duty and was happy to pass on the responsibility.

"No, Patrick, I believe he's in your station this evening," I responded, rolling my eyes. I was getting tired of this joke.

"No really, Phoebe, Mr. Bruni's on table six." He was serious, and I was seriously going to throw up. At that moment, I had *Food & Wine* doing a VIP menu on table three, the Zagats doing their usual abbreviated, high-maintenance menu on table four, and was trying to turn table five for some guy who had just written a biography of some restaurateur (I had been too busy to pay attention when the maître d' gave me the details only moments before).

I peered around the corner into the dining room. Sure enough, there was Frank. *Food & Wine* faded in my mind; someone else could coddle the Zagats. This was the moment we had been waiting for. Technically, this could be his last visit, as most reviewers visit a restaurant three times or so.

André poured champagne and I explained the menus to the guests, positioning myself directly opposite so I could make easy eye contact with Mr. Bruni. He was much more relaxed this evening, and I began to have fun as well. He and the other gentleman at the table ordered the vegetable menu, while the two ladies had the chef's tasting menu with the foie gras torchon, a reversal of the norm. The evening was fairly uneventful (in the best of senses) until the cheese course. I had just served the cheese and was describing the Tarentaise cheese from Vermont when one of the women at the table enthusiastically exclaimed, "Oh, Tarentaise, we wrote about this cheese!" and then, realizing that I would most likely have seen the huge wheel of Tarentaise on the cover of the *New York Times* food section the week before, clapped her hand over her mouth.

"Right," I answered, pausing, and trying not to laugh. But everyone else at the table cracked up, and I resumed my explanation, knowing that he knew that I knew and that he knew that I knew that he knew.

Relaxed, confident, and relieved to be nearing the end of

Bruni's meal, I began to make the arrangements for a final surprise course. The "Michael Jackson" chocolate presentation was named after the single white glove one originally wore to pick up individual chocolates. There were six rows in total, two rows of milk, dark, and white, from which the guests were invited to select as many as they wished. Billy, one of our most knowledgeable food runners, stood across the table from Mr. Bruni with the tray, as we had discussed, so he could make eye contact and have the best view. Billy went through all thirty chocolates, explaining some of the more esoteric flavors such as verjus (unfermented grape juice), fenugreek, Chimay beer, and smoked chocolate ganache. At the end of the presentation, the guests all looked a little hesitant and overwhelmed, and I thought I might step in to offer a little guidance. After all, we had just spent quite a few hours together, everything seemed to be going along just swimmingly, why not offer a little friendly advice?

"The question is, really," I began, "do you want something experimental or something a little more down-home country?"

As soon as the words left my lips, time seemed to slow like a decelerating LP. *Down-home country?* I had never uttered the phrase in my life. Billy, still bent over the table's edge with his gloved hand hovering over the large silver tray, turned his head slowly toward me with a look of both horror and amusement.

"What exactly would constitute a 'down-home country' chocolate, Phoebe?" Billy asked, the corners of his lips holding back his generous and familiar grin.

I blathered for a moment about "comforting" flavors such as hazelnut, peanut butter, and coffee, and moved as quickly as I could away from the table. From that moment on, I wished on every eyelash, star, and graveyard that I would not live to see that phrase in print, even if it meant hurling myself from the highest silo or hayloft I could find.

I DIDN'T TELL anyone about the down-home incident—not even André. He had seen the whole exchange, but was too far away to hear. André had it easy these days; his was the one department that seemed to be off the hook. Mr. Bruni himself wasn't all that interested in discussing wine, so he either brought someone else who ordered or he left the selection to the sommeliers. Of course, the sommeliers needed to be on time and on point with their pairings, but the place was teeming with managers eager to lend a hand. The one person who was not off the hook was André.

"Don't leave, okay?" I said to him.

"Chef, there's nowhere I'd rather be."

"Because the next course is coming up and I am going to have to get the markings down, plus more bread and the glasses, and pour the wine, and I already see them plating—"

"Would you calm down?"

If there was one thing I admired about André, it was his ability to keep a cool head in a time of crisis. When things became heated, André was the one who ignored the commotion and made sure things got back on track. He picked up the food when the chef started hollering; he marked the table when the food was in the breezeway and the backserver was nowhere to be found; he went and got the two bottles a guest was choosing between so that by the time the order was eventually placed, both wines were sitting on the captain's station. If there was one person I could trust to know when I needed help and when I had it under control, it was André.

He and I had been spending more and more time together. We

met after work, and when we had days off together, we fled to Brooklyn, where we were almost sure not to run into anyone.

"So what's the story with you and Leigh?" I asked on one of these days. We were eating brunch in Williamsburg at one of the many retro-chic diners that charge eight dollars for a side of polenta. "Shit," a friend exclaimed one night when looking at a similar menu. "Them's some pricey-ass grits!"

"What do you mean 'what's the story'?" I was beginning to notice that André often answered a question only after repeating it at least once. Maybe it was like an anxious speller at a bee trying to buy time by asking for the word to be repeated. Then asking for its definition. Then asking for its derivation.

"What are you doing with me when you're living with someone else?"

"It's over," he answered with a slight shrug and a shake of his head.

"Does she know that?"

"What do you mean 'does she know that'? I told her it was over before we even moved to New York."

"So why did you move together?"

This time he didn't even repeat the question, he just shrugged again. When I pressed, he told me that she hadn't wanted to move to New York at all. So far, her opinion of the city as cold and difficult had been confirmed. It didn't help that they had few friends here. And, unlike André, she had never been a big nightlife person, so they had been spending more and more time apart. It was clear that André didn't want to go further into it, and I let it go. This short conversation put my conscience at ease—not because I believed that it was really over, but because I now had an excuse. I could honestly look wide-eyed at a potential accuser and claim innocence.

"It's a disaster waiting to happen," I bragged to some

friends from the old café job. "I'll give it to the end of the summer." We were lounging in hammocks and garden chairs behind the Park Slope brownstone where one of them lived. The hostess was half Greek and half German, so there was yogurt, walnuts, and honey as well as sausages and dark, heavy breads. The last time I visited this particular garden, the summery ankle-length dress that I had borrowed from a friend (a dramatic number featuring alternating panels of solid primary colors and floating hot-air balloons) got a little too cozy with a candle by my feet and went up in flames. I only noticed when my friend Sylvia began waving her arms and swearing in Spanish before dousing me with sangria. The high school sweetheart, who still lived downstairs from me at this point, heroically attempted to come to my rescue, but became tangled in his hammock and ended up rolling himself up in it "like a burrito," Sylvia described later. My life was spared by a chef who, amid the hysteria, calmly wrung the flames out like a dishtowel.

Alas, no one could rescue me from my current predicament with André. The joke was on me. At first it was funny that he had programmed my name as "Patrick" in his phone. Who cared what he told Leigh the first night he didn't go home? I didn't even mind the thought that he might still be in love with her. And then, suddenly, I did.

Here I was, falling in love with a man who, for all I knew, had a penchant for infidelity. I took psychology freshman year in college; I had read Freud and Jung and *Madame Bovary* and half of the books in the self-help and relationship sections. I knew that it wasn't coincidence that my parents had recently performed a drama with similar acts. With horror, I considered I was the "other woman" in this modern remake. What would Freud have to say about that? Maybe I wanted to know just how easy it was to cheat. Maybe I wanted to prove that commitment and monogamy weren't possible, that my parents hadn't lied when they said "till death do us part." Or maybe I just liked to win.

"I think you should stop seeing me and try to make it work with Leigh," I told André in the first of what would be many hand-wringing sessions. We had met after work at a nearby pub we recently discovered no one else frequented.

"Whatever." He took a swig of his beer and pretended to watch the game.

"No, I'm serious. I think we should stop seeing each other and you should really try to fix things. Seven years! That's something worth salvaging."

He fixed his gaze on the television screen as I spoke, but then turned to face me. "Listen, cut the bullshit. If you want us to stop seeing each other, that's fine. But Leigh and I are not getting back together."

I would come to this junction again and again over the next few months. Either I refused to see André until he and Leigh had officially split and I could be sure that it was really over or I continued to see him and hoped he would straighten it out before I died of guilt poisoning.

"You just have to trust me," he said.

At that point, the conversation ended abruptly. One of the sous chefs and two cooks had just walked in. While they settled into three stools and leaned around one another to see what was on tap, I took the opportunity to slip out the side door. There was Leigh to think about, but more important, there was the fact that, as a manager, André was technically not supposed to date one of the staff. The longer we could keep this under wraps, the better.

Any reluctance I had was soon wooed and won over and we

found ways to amuse ourselves in corners of the city where we would go unseen—dusty corners that Giuliani forgot to clean, corner banquettes behind pillars and plants. Perhaps the epitome of this grand posture of discretion was the night we checked into the Plaza. Rumor had it that the famous hotel was closing, ostensibly for renovation. I feared that meant closing and reopening without soul or charm. There was a simple reason for my attachment to this particular hotel: it was the setting for the children's book *Eloise*. As a kid, I wore household objects as hats, just like Eloise. I made a great production out of yawning. I was also equally indulged—not by bell captains and valets (for Lord's sake) but by my New York–born mother and aunts. I spent hours tracing the dotted red lines that charted Eloise's scamperings throughout the hotel in which she lived with her English nanny, her sneaker-wearing turtle, Skipperdee, and her dog, Weenie. After each reading, I swore to my mother that I simply had to move there as soon as possible.

André, who had not grown up fantasizing about ordering a single strawberry leaf and two raisins from room service, only feigned remorse when I delivered the news. He started to grasp the depth of my grief, however, when I announced that I had booked us a room on his next day off.

The hotel was within walking distance of André's apartment and a subway ride from mine, so there was no real need to pack. We met near work to buy a little wine and walk over together. In keeping with his usual good-natured nonchalance, André arrived in sneakers and announced that there was only one thing he needed to accomplish that day.

"Chef, I'm going to need to get me a ham."

"A ham. . . ."

"And some mustard."

Absurd as this sounded, I remembered that André had made mention of ham a few days before. We were standing in the dining room, our gazes on the tables, when he described the craving. He was unusually impassioned and proceeded, throughout the shift, to disseminate the importance of glazes and nations of origin. Later in the evening, when I stopped at the bar to pick up some drinks, I discovered that I wasn't the only one to whom André confessed his longings.

"What's with André and the ham?" the bartender had asked. I just shook my head.

In restaurants, because of the many distractions, conversations often last an entire shift. A question asked when grabbing a bottle of water from the fridge is answered after clearing a table, and then commented on an hour later when inputting something in the computer. That night, ham had been one such topic.

We walked up to Citarella, the gourmet food shop at Broadway and Seventy-fifth, and grabbed a nice, rosy round of pork the size of a volleyball and a few jars of mustard: Dijon to be safe, stone-ground for texture, and tarragon for variety. Then we bought a few bottles of wine, not knowing our mood.

It was clear why the Plaza decided to renovate. Paint chipped from the walls, carpets frayed at the edges, and worn knobs and buttons showed their age. André looked around, unimpressed. This was far from the travel magazine spread he had imagined. To me, it was like an aging movie star, still elegant, but only a reminder of what it had once been. The gentleman at the front desk asked whether we needed help with our bags. I looked over at André, who was standing in the marble lobby beside an enormous bouquet of white lilies, holding a grocery bag. He jutted out his chin, as if to ask whether I needed something and I shook my head in return.

"That won't be necessary."

After we had found our room, nondescript and slightly stale, we put on two white robes and I told André to get comfortable. I took out my yellowed and stained copy of *Eloise*, the same one I packed when I moved to New York for college and in every move since, and began to read. André laughed at all the right places and when we were done, I think he had more appreciation for our surroundings. We opened a bottle of Pinot Gris, popped the mustard, and unwrapped the ham. We hadn't thought to bring a knife, so I called room service, who brought a dull butter knife. The blade on André's wine key sufficed for a while, but in the end we just tore it with our fingers.

"You have to eat ham or you'll dry up," I told André, revising one of my favorite lines from the book to fit the occasion.

"Everyone knows that," he answered.

ANDRÉ TOLD ME to have patience, and I didn't have to wait long. He and Leigh had it out at the end of the summer. At the same time, the story leaked among the ladies of Per Se. Soon, when I walked into the women's locker room, conversations stopped. I was obviously not welcome to eat dinner in the little nook where a posse of women runners and backservers often sat. If my coworkers had been any less professional, none of the guests in my station would ever have gotten their food and my backservers would have left me to fend for myself. But they performed their jobs as perfectly as they always had. The only change was that I was invisible. I couldn't blame them. It wasn't as if I were being persecuted for something noble or courageous.

Leigh left the restaurant toward the end of the summer. It wasn't going to work for all three of us to be there. She continued to live with André, presumably looking for her own place. The situation irked me more than I let on, but André and I agreed not to talk about it. I had made my point about needing to clean up whatever mess we had created in his life. He made his point about my having to trust him and the fact that he was taking care of it. In some ways, it was a relief that she knew. No more dive bars or luxury hotels for us; we were ready to paint the town.

But first we had to get André a MetroCard. Having spent most of his first five months setting up the wine cellar, André's stomping grounds had about a ten-block radius. He walked to work in the morning, went to the gym in the basement of the building, and walked home from work late. From what I gathered, he even spent a majority of his days off at work. Every so often he had a beer and a burger at a pub or late-night restaurant, but he took cabs to these.

I, on the other hand, had lived in New York for eight years and was no stranger to the subway, but had always felt a little out of the loop. Fortunately, I could take comfort in my suspicion that most people who live in New York feel a little out of one loop or another. What passes for fashion in the East Village looks like a Halloween costume on the Upper East Side. When I lived in Williamsburg, the hipster uniform was something like a floral thrift-store dress dating anywhere from the 1940s to the 1970s worn over jeans or with vintage heels, or the 1980s look: thick belt, off-the-shoulder shirt, leg warmers, and Converse sneakers. But once the subway doors closed and whisked the hipster under the river, she would be bait for ridicule. Residents of multimillion-dollar lofts in SoHo might think her grungy. The reluctantly retired executive Upper East Side mother, looking out the window of her navy blue Suburban, might wonder where one even finds an outfit like that. The professor and the therapist on the Upper West Side might consider, respectively, the amount of time wasted putting the look together and what she was trying to say with it. The fact that she would even find herself in the Financial District seems unlikely, but if so, she would be a splash of color in a sea of suits. In Harlem, she would be accused of driving up the rents; and in Chelsea, the land of the big man with a little dog, she would go completely unseen. This, my friends, is why everyone in New York wears black. Think of it as a sliding-scale uniform, with black Old Navy T-shirts on one end and black Prada boots on the other.

I had been paralyzed by all of this for eight years, but things were about to change. I now had at my side the well-dressed and unfazeable André; I had extra cash for the first time in a while; and I knew how to use a fish knife if put on the spot. After years of reading about New York while living in New York, I was ready to plunge.

On work nights, André and I were hindered by time. There were only a few restaurants still serving after I changed my last tablecloth. When we were off, the city, which had never been my friend, now put its bejeweled arm over my shoulder and smiled conspiringly. I usually picked the restaurants because I subscribed to just about every food publication out there and had a long list of places to try. But André was soon compiling his own list. For the first year at Per Se, there was almost always a chef, restaurant owner, or maître d' from another restaurant in our dining room. Better yet, line cooks and waiters. By the end of these services, we had promised to stop in on our next day off.

Often on our way to dinner, we popped in to say hello to one of these new acquaintances, an old coworker of mine, or a new contact of André's. Sometimes we got out after one drink, but more often than not, a little something would come from the kitchen. It was only polite to protest, and only polite to clean the plate. When a chef sends something from the kitchen, it is often one of the best things on the menu or something new that he's working on. After paying the check, or leaving an extravagant tip when there was no check, we set out again in the direction of dinner. But wasn't there a new place right near here that we had heard about? We stopped there and perhaps ordered an appetizer or two. By the time we got to our final destination, we were far from hungry, but still curious. On nights like these, we usually chose to sit at the bar, where we felt comfortable ordering only a few dishes.

I had been meaning to check out a place on Elizabeth Street, and when I heard they had opened a little wine bar underneath the restaurant, I moved it to the top of my restaurant list. On our next day off, we headed to SoHo and strolled for a while, reading menus and comparing tastes in shoes and ties and baubles in the windows. I slid my arm around André's waist and hooked my thumb in his jean pocket. I had only to take a slightly larger step to match his stride.

We decided to stop in the restaurant's new bar for a glass of wine before dinner. If it hadn't been for the Beach Boys album playing, the cavernous basement might have felt a little creepy. Dark wood and ironwork gave the room a gothic feel, and, like most basements, this one had the cold, damp climate proven ideal for bogeymen. It was genius really, because the room made me want to cozy up to one of the many candles and warm myself with a glass of something rustic and heartening. We nibbled on a few breadsticks with our wine, but hunger soon nudged us from our wooden stools and back up the stone stairs toward the main dining room. As we climbed out, André grabbed my arm.

"That's the kind of dog I've always wanted," he said, pointing to a four-legged animal the size and heft of a fire hydrant. It was breathing like Darth Vader after a flight of stairs. "I love those dogs."

Evidently, Buckwheat was a French bulldog who belonged to the chef and sort of ran things around the place. Although he did not correspond to my particular aesthetic sensibilities, after a moment's consideration, I realized that I should be excited that André even liked dogs.

"My, what big ears you have!" I cooed, scratching Buckwheat between his big bat ears. It was hard to believe that this creature had descended from a wolf.

As I explained when we reached our table, I wasn't used to small city dogs. I had grown up with a "real dog," a collie/golden retriever named Turnip.

"She had a nose and everything!" I told André.

"Buckwheat's a real dog." He sounded offended. "And he has a nose—it's just a little smooshed."

"Do you have pets?"

"No, we left Leigh's cat back in Texas."

Oops, wrong turn. I was considering how to get us back on track, but André spoke first.

"Ever heard that thing about porn star names—how they're supposed to be the name of your first pet and the name of the street where you grew up?"

"Really? Okay, let's see . . . Turnip White-Hollow."

"That's hot."

"You're telling me you'd really want to sleep with someone named after a root vegetable?"

"Oh, yeah."

"Rutabaga?"

"No. But Rhubarb, maybe."

"Did you have pets as a kid?"

"No, Leigh's cat was the first. I'd be Maxwell Montgomery."

"You'd make millions." Eager to move away from Leigh and porn, I went back to canines. "I kind of like dachshunds. I like their Romanesque profiles."

"We're not getting a dachshund."

We? As in a *we* that might live in a town house in the West Village with a wine cellar/cheese cave, an herb garden, and a red library with a sliding ladder? I tried to appear unfazed.

"Come on, we'll name him some old-man name like George or Stanley and dress him in little argyle sweaters and yellow raincoats." André looked at me blankly for a moment and then picked up the wine list.

"White or red? Or bubbles?"

"I don't know, what are we eating?"

After only a few meals together, we had already established a routine. André would start in on the wine list while I scoured the menu. We then peppered each other with questions, although not really listening or expecting an answer.

"Should we start with white? Or a glass of champagne?"

"What do you think of cocoa nibs and preserved lemon together?"

"We should drink red."

"Why do all restaurants have the same salad?"

After an initial read-through, André closed the wine list and picked up the menu.

"What looks good?"

This was my cue to take it from the top. My first rule in dining out is to avoid the following: tuna tartare, fried calamari, mixed greens, tomato and mozzarella, Caesar salad, roast or grilled chicken, blackened or poached salmon, crab cakes, and the requisite steak. I have nothing against any of these dishes, but when I go out, I don't want something that (a) even I can make and (b) I have had a million times. André's one exception to this rule was his personal holy grail: the perfect burger.

My second rule of dining is never to order the same thing as anyone else in the party unless he or she is ill or stingy. I tended toward rabbit, lamb, anything with polenta, anything with eggs, and esoteric flavor combinations. André gravitated in the direction of sweetbreads, duck, bacon, pork, anything with truffles, and anything involving sausage. No sea urchin for me. No coconut for him. It went without saying that the kitschiest item on the menu deserved a chance—sweetbread poppers, fried pickles, fried Mars bars, grits, mac and cheese, fried chicken, creamed spinach, and deviled eggs. When the waiter arrived, pad in hand, I had the final say on the menu and André ordered the wine he wanted to drink. He knew I liked sparkling water. I knew he needed the salt close at hand.

After ordering, we turned our attention to the restaurant, pointing out all of the bad tables in the room and scrutinizing the uniforms. Just thinking about my uniform made my throat constrict and my feet sweat, despite my minimalist black tank top and strappy heels, which were a far cry from the Town Car shoes.

André made one comment in almost every place we went.

"If I were going to own a restaurant, it would look something like this."

"Hmmm. As opposed to the wine bar last week?"

"Anyways," he answered. It was an affectionate André-ism, signifying the end of a discussion, and one I was beginning to love.

· A TIP ·

Don't send something back after eating most of it.

• the fault, dear bruni •

tHERE HE WAS again.

"Good to see you again, sir," I greeted Mr. Bruni on his fourth visit.

"I was just thinking about you the other day!" he answered. He was sitting on table three with someone who, from the ease with which they were chatting, appeared to be a good friend. I pretended to blush. "Wait—no—not like that. . . ."

He explained that he was thinking about how intensely I had been staring at him during his last visit, while he ate the risotto. Great, I thought to myself. He thinks I'm creepy. What about the managers hiding behind the flower arrangements, weren't they creepy? What about Gabriel, who had been standing alongside me throughout the meal?

"Should we pour him more water?"

"No, don't cramp him."

"Okay, I'll let him take a few more sips."

"Oh, wait [elbow, elbow], he just chugged it. Go pour."

"No—you go, I was just there."

"His wine is low, too. Don't let him pour."

"Should I take the bottle off the table?"

"Best not to take a chance."

"Did you hear what he just said?"

"No, but I think it was something about the fish. Should I go say something?"

And so on.

I will admit, I had been staring at him, but only because I wanted to know whether he agreed with me that the truffle risotto was close to perfection. I had also been thinking about something that occurred earlier in the evening, before the risotto, and before the "down-home country" incident. Although he and his guests were firm in their resolve to order from the menu, the kitchen had slipped in a custard course as an extra canapé. As he picked up his custard spoon, I noticed that he paused and looked down at his scrambled hen egg with truffle coulis, seeming perplexed.

"You look perplexed," I observed.

"I am. What makes these scrambled eggs any different from my scrambled eggs? Why would a restaurant of this caliber serve a whole course revolving around eggs?"

I thought about this for a moment. He was right, really. I had never thought to question the custard course. Some of the more virtuosic egg preparations seemed more appropriate: the white truffle-infused custard served in an eggshell or the pickled hen egg with truffle filling made to look like a deviled egg and paired with a tiny truffle "Pop-Tart." But a soft-boiled, scrambled, or coddled egg was simply an egg, no matter how much truffle coulis you added.

I dodged the question, babbling instead about the rabbi from whom we bought our eggs and the benefits of a Bonnet stove. When I finally extricated myself from the table, I went straight to the kitchen, where Corey was in the throes of service.

"Why do we serve eggs?" I asked.

"What do you mean, 'why do we serve eggs'?" he responded irritably, stirring something violently over the stove by the pass.

"I mean, what makes them so special that we would do an entire course around them?" I realized that this was a bad time, but hoped that he might have something I could take back to the table with me.

"Because they are eggs! Eggs! Do you think we could have this conversation another time?"

I went back to the dining room with nothing. Clearly, I wasn't going to go to the table and tell Frank Bruni that we served eggs because they were eggs. I let the question go unanswered and concentrated on more concrete tasks.

In the days following, I tried to outline a thoughtful response for Mr. Bruni, should he come back. After a little digging, I came across an essay by Michelle Wildgen in *Tin House* titled "Ode to an Egg." In it, I found references to Hemingway's characters eating eggs in such a way as to foretell their fate. A few lines later, came a magical quote by M. F. K. Fisher: "Probably one of the most private things in the world is an egg until it is broken." I read musings on the sound of the word *egg*, on its shape, and on its meaning: "At times I think the nutmeg speckling on a blue egg is as much as we can hope for." Perhaps the best lines in the piece were her last: "The egg is drama and succor, birth and parenthood, sex and death, the start and the finish. The egg is inevitable." I photocopied the essay for those in my life who would appreciate it. I even left a copy on Corey's desk. But would I be able to convey any of this to Mr. Bruni?

"I've been considering what you said about the scrambled eggs," I told him on his next visit. Although I couldn't really explain why the egg deserved its own course, I believed wholeheartedly that it did, if only for its solitary perfection. He nodded and seemed to agree, but he might have been humoring me.

Not surprisingly, Corey and I never discussed the drama and succor of the inevitable egg. It was just my luck that almost every time Mr. Bruni came in, Corey was expediting in the kitchen. In some ways, I felt as if I had critics on both fronts. In other ways, I felt that Corey and I were partners whether we liked it or not. Especially in times like these, with so much at stake, it is easy to lose touch with the symbiotic relationship between front and back of the house. From my perspective, the review would be about the food; there was only so much spin I could put on a lukewarm cobia or the world's best scrambled eggs. According to the kitchen, however, there was quite a bit I could do to screw it up.

Per Se had no cameras in the dining room, and the chefs had to rely on my observations and the truth of a clean plate. God help the captain or runner who returned to the kitchen holding a plate with food left over and could not give a satisfying explanation as to why it was not finished. Each time I returned with plates, I found the expectant and terrified eyes of Corey or J.B., and certainly of the chef de partie of that particular station. When the fish plates came back, it was the fish cook who was standing on his tiptoes to see the plate; when meat came back not entirely finished, it was the meat cook who picked up the scraps and squeezed them to feel if they were overcooked.

There was no meat to be squeezed or any other major upsets during Mr. Bruni's fourth visit. It was a shorter meal because he and his friend ordered from the five-course menu and requested not to be sent anything other than what they ordered. It seemed that he was really trying to experience the restaurant as an average guest. They spoke mainly to each other, and asked only a few questions about the food. Even so, I analyzed every comment and gesture. I watched Mr. Bruni read the menu; I watched his face as he ate; I watched where his eyes fell and what caught his interest in the dining room. I studied his credit card, on which the name Dirk McKenzie appeared, and wondered if he built different personas around each of his identities. The more I watched Frank Bruni, the more fixated I became. I recently read in a study that people who watch a lot of television believe they have more friends than those who don't. The more a face becomes familiar, the closer you feel to that person, even if they show up once a week behind a square piece of glass.

"You're scaring me," André said that night as I went over Mr. McKenzie's dinner in minute detail. "They're only stars."

"Only stars? You are so clearly not from New York." Neither was I, for that matter, but I loved it more. But maybe he was right. I needed to put this whole review thing out of my mind for a while.

MY COUSIN OWEN was getting married in Vermont, so I asked André if he'd like to go. Even though we were free to roam the city together these days, I still had pangs of guilt when he went home at six in the morning. Was Leigh staring at the ceiling, unable to sleep? Would she even ask where he had been? It would be a relief to have some time together in another setting.

"It'll be great. We can stay in a little bed-and-breakfast and eat pancakes. There'll be cows!"

"We have cows in Texas, you know," he said. But he agreed to go, and I reserved us a rental car.

We would drive up early on Saturday morning on the day of the wedding, and drive back the next day, in time for both of us to work dinner. It wasn't much time, but compared to the hours both of us usually worked, it was a long weekend. At three o'clock in the morning on Saturday, André called.

"Why are you whispering?" I asked, trying to wake up enough to make sense out of his call.

"I'm in the bathroom."

"Whose bathroom?" Now I was awake.

He slurred something about being at a party and having found a car for us to borrow.

"Don't drive!" I yelled into the phone. I was sitting stark naked on the arm of my couch by the window where the reception was better.

After we hung up, I sent him a text message suggesting that we meet at my favorite bakery on Columbus at ten and pick up the car together. I figured that, not being too far from his apartment, it was fairly hangover-proof.

I got there early, as I tend to do, and considered my options if he didn't show. I don't drive, so renting a car by myself was out. I suppose there was always a bus, but that would be tight. I called. No answer. I left a message asking where he was.

"On my way," he wrote in a text message. I went outside to wait.

Because I had no idea what kind of car to look for, I didn't notice the white minivan pull up at 10:30 until I heard honking. André waved and grinned from the window. He was wearing his picnic basket shirt and looked a little like a soccer dad whose other car was something small and red. I grabbed my turquoise hatbox by its plastic looped handle and crossed the street to meet André. I bought that hatbox at a thrift store in Williamsburg after envisioning just such an occasion.

"Leigh said to tell you hello," André said as I climbed into the front seat.

"Well, that was nice of her."

"Actually she hollered it from the window when I was half-way down the block."

"Ah." I strapped myself in. "But here you are. How'd you score the wheels?"

"It's my wine rep's mother's car. We had dinner at some guy's house last night. I think they were supposed to be having a date, but the date kept talking to his sister and my rep kept talking to me."

"She probably wants to sleep with you."

"You think?" He looked over at me and winked. "Too bad I'm taken."

"And then some," I said with a dramatic roll of my eyes and turned around to see if the mother of the woman who wanted to sleep with my boyfriend had a map somewhere.

With our late start and the miles to cover, we would barely make the wedding. I called the bed-and-breakfast in Brattle-boro where I had made a reservation and told them that we would have to check in that night. It was late summer and it seemed that the farther we drove from Manhattan's gray sky-line, the roads just kept getting smaller and the trees greener. The town where Owen, his future bride, and their baby had settled was barely even a town. I would call it a village, a ham-let, or maybe just a few people and a post office.

"There's a bunch of cars in the driveway of that house," I said as we drove over a single-lane bridge.

"Which house?"

By the time I turned around to point, we had reached the

end of the town. We went back and parked near the other cars. At the top of a little hill was a big red barn and tucked against the side of the hill, a tent. I climbed into the back of the van and put on the red taffeta dress that I had found at another thrift shop in Williamsburg. It seemed like festive wedding attire when I had tried it on at home, but I now had second thoughts. I had forgotten, once again, that this was the land of round-toed shoes and earth tones. I was wearing pointy black boots with my red taffeta. André looked dapper, as always, in his tweed jacket and brown loafers without socks. Suddenly, it occurred to me that he was about to meet my family. I hadn't really thought about that.

Owen wore a green velvet suit and top hat that he bought on eBay. Laura was barefoot in white. They took turns holding the baby throughout the ceremony and then danced with her when the bluegrass band started playing. At one point, I looked over at André, who was happily drinking his organic beer and laughing with my brother, and marveled at how comfortable he was in this scene. To me, an outdoor hippie wedding was normal. Hummus was my first food. But for someone who grew up on military bases eating Texas portions of red meat, this was a different planet. But the only thing he seemed to find odd was how many Subarus he saw on the road.

After the wedding, we checked into our bed-and-breakfast. Ours was the Blue Room at the top of the stairs. It was blue. Although it was still early and the Brattleboro nightlife was just getting started, we put on the white robes that had been laid out for us and listened to the quiet.

The next day, our drive was slightly more leisurely, although we both had to be at work by the dinner shift. The wedding had me thinking about families. We talked about mine and my parents' divorce. André had met my father briefly at the wedding, but my mother didn't come. He talked about his mother's big family and the death of his stepfather. Leigh came up a few times.

"Why do you think it didn't work out between you two?" I asked.

He didn't respond right away, and I wondered if he had heard me or whether he was choosing not to answer the question. When he did respond, he answered a different question altogether.

"Leigh taught me how to love."

There was such tenderness in the way he said this, as if he had no interest in revisiting the negative parts of their relationship. As I would discover, he chose never to say anything negative about any of his past girlfriends. That meant I never got to gloat, but it also showed me that he was careful with people, as if he wanted to respect the privacy of their relationship even now that it had ended.

We left the little roads and bridges behind us and joined the masses elbowing their way through tunnels and over bridges to get into the city.

"Look!" I said to André when the skyline came into view. "We live there!"

"I know," he answered with a touch of pride.

Even if we lived in different boroughs, I liked that we called the same place home.

YOU'VE GOT TO be kidding, I thought to myself. Again?

One of the managers poured Mr. Bruni some champagne, and I approached his table once more, with two menus under my arm.

"Do you ever get a day off?" he asked before introducing his guest.

I had now waited on him, in some capacity, on four occasions. If he were the average guest, he would be a regular. I decided to treat him as such. We chatted about our favorite restaurants in the city, and about some of the dishes he had enjoyed at Per Se. Toward the end of the meal, I asked whether we could expect to see him again, figuring that he could answer vaguely if he wished to continue the facade. To my surprise, he answered as himself.

"I think I have played favoritism enough. Usually I go to a place three or four times. I have been here six."

Six? We had only counted five. After a few more questions, it was clear that he had been in during our first weeks of service.

"I sat right here," he said, reaching up to the second level and grabbing the leg of the chair by his head.

"How was it?" I had to ask, but was afraid to hear his answer.

"Let's just say you've worked out a lot of the kinks."

It was a heartfelt good-bye, at least on my part. I thanked him for making what could have been a horrendously stressful process a lot of fun. He said he had looked forward to his visits and would miss coming back.

"He's going to miss coming back!" I squealed as I tore back into the kitchen. Corey rolled his eyes, but I knew he was ecstatic.

A few days later, I was walking through the kitchen on my way to set up the dining room. I was a little early and the kitchen was quiet, each cook silently prepping for service. Corey was at the pass, wrapping some square piece of meat in caul fat. I wanted to ask what it was exactly but was not really up to the challenge of conversation. But that day it was Corey who spoke first.

"Hey," he called out just as I was about to round the corner into the breezeway, "have you talked to your friend Frank lately?"

"No, I think I will wait to call until after the review."

Corey looked shocked. "I was joking. Are you seriously going to call him?"

I explained that I wanted to do a stage, as it is called in chef's parlance. A stage is an unpaid apprenticeship in a kitchen—or in my case, a dining room. Corey looked horrified.

"Is that what you really want to do? Review?" I could tell that if I had ever had the chance to win an ounce of favor with him, I had just blown it. He went on a long tirade about how little reviewers know about food, how unfair it is to a restaurant to base everything on one person's opinion. I nodded and scratched my head, not telling him that these were the same fears I had myself when I considered the career. At the end of his speech, he sighed and went back to the sheets of caul fat in front of him that looked like sturdy cobwebs. As our conversation appeared to be over, I turned once again toward the breezeway where my colleagues would soon congregate to gossip about last night's juicy escapades.

"So what you are saying is"—apparently the conversation was not finished—"some day I am going to hear that you are sitting in my restaurant and really wish I had been nicer to you?" I could barely see the grin, as his head was bent over his task, but I could hear it in his voice.

"Pretty much, yeah." For one moment, I felt as if I had won. And then, realizing that he had just let me win, braced myself.

EVERY WEEK, STARTING in the middle of July, we were convinced was the week the review would come out. The *Times* usually calls sometime over the weekend to arrange for photographers to come before the review appears in Wednesday's "Dining Out" section. There was a growing suspicion that it would come out after our assumed clientele moved back from the Hamptons or flew in from late summer weeks in Monaco. But then there were a million theories floating around. Mr. Bruni had bumped Bouley down to three stars, with the chilling comment that he had "the sense of being at a party to which I had come too late, or at which I had stayed too long." Although there isn't a four-star-restaurant quota, the demotion of Bouley seemed to leave a spot wide open for another restaurant of American cuisine and French influence. On the other hand, it was rare for any restaurant to open with four stars.

We received the call in the first week of September and immediately began preparing the room for the photographers.

"It must be *pristine!*" Paolo, our Italian manager, called out, pronouncing *pristine* so it rhymed with *feline*. He circled the dining room, calling out what were apparently supposed to be inspirational words—"world-class!"—while frantically folding and refolding napkins, holding wineglasses up to the light, and measuring the angles of all the lamp shades. "I invite you to polish all the surfaces." Accent on the second syllable of *surfaces*.

In the end, the photographers rearranged everything in order to get shots of the plates against certain backgrounds. They took some pictures during service as well, but none of this mattered to me. I had no interest in being the face of Per Se, and, in fact, I had a feeling that they would choose their standard dining room shot and maybe a few of the food. I was much more worried about what Mr. Bruni had to say and whether it would include the phrase "down-home country." Okay, so there is no "I" in team and all that jazz, but I had waited on Mr. Bruni in some capacity four of the six times he ate at Per

Se, and if he had something negative to say about service, you had better believe all eyes would look my way.

We held our collective breath until Tuesday night. It is a tradition for the *New York Times* critic to give a synopsis of the review on New York 1 News at about 9:20 P.M. on Tuesday night. In these clips, they carefully block out his face to maintain his anonymity, as if he were in some sort of gastronomic witness protection program. That night we had our preservice meeting as usual, all of us fidgeting through what were supposed to be encouraging speeches about continuing to set our own standards and not letting the review go to our heads, no matter how many stars. I chewed on ice from a Styrofoam coffee cup. The director of operations chewed his lower lip.

Sometime between six and seven that evening, when the dining room was about half full, my party of six arrived. In the party was none other than William Grimes, the previous *Times* reviewer. Either we had nothing to worry about, I thought to myself, or Mr. Grimes did.

I was in the kitchen a little after eight o'clock when Chef Keller breezed in from the airport wearing his usual California-casual attire and chef clogs. He was holding a printout of the review above his head and grinning.

"Congratulations!" he called out. The kitchen froze. "Four stars!"

The kitchen and breezeway erupted into four-star mayhem, kisses and congratulations flowing freely. As it turned out, Thomas happened to be walking in through the back of the restaurant just as the baker saw it come out online. It was a fittingly dramatic entrance and for a moment, we forgot everything else. Since everyone was kissing everyone, I went and found André, who was standing by the wine cellar.

"Still in service, people!" someone shouted above the din, reminding us to pick up the food that had been momentarily forgotten on the pass, to refill water glasses that had been drained while we were dancing in the back. Chef Keller insisted that we pour champagne for everyone in the dining room and quite a few of us stopped by Mr. Grimes's table, hoping that he would pass along our thanks to his colleague at the *Times*.

As soon as we finished our tables in the dining room, we were told to head to the large private room in the back where everyone would convene. I was one of the last to be finished and when I got there, the room was packed. Staff members who were not working had rushed over from bars and living rooms where they had been glued to New York 1 and were earnestly shaking one another's hands. All the chefs, still in their blue aprons, and the floor staff, still in our black suits, filled the room. There was a jeroboam of Veuve Clicquot and the largest tin of caviar I have ever seen. Thomas gave a speech commending everyone and encouraging us to continue setting our own goals and standards. "Next is *Mobil Travel Guide* five stars," he added with a gleam in his eye.

The few staff who did not make it over to the party met us downtown, where the restaurant had rented out the top floor of a bar. One of the captains arrived with a huge stack of papers and we all tried, fairly unsuccessfully, to read over one another's shoulders, cocktails balanced precariously on borrowed limbs. Looking around, I realized that it was one of the few times since orientation that we had all been together: early-morning prep cooks, hosts and reservationists, sommeliers, captains, backservers, kitchen servers, bartenders, bakers. Of course, as we had all just worked a long, tense shift and were expected to provide four-star service the next day as well, the crowd thinned toward the early-morning hours. Gabriel, Patrick, André, Mandy, and I all slid into empty seats, put our feet up, and grinned at one another. It was finally calm enough to read the review all the way through. Patrick's line about the rabbit made it in, and much to my relief, "down-home country" did not. It would be some time before I would be able to tell anyone about that. Besides the rabbit comment, which was only one example of the "cheeky banter" Bruni encountered during his visits, service only got one real line: "I am handicapped slightly in evaluating the service," the review read, "because the vigilant staff repeatedly recognized me and kept a special watch over my table."

One lousy line for all of that?

In the end, what convinced him of our worth was the simple elegance of the vegetable tasting menu. I remembered watching him as he ate the truffle risotto and the look of amusement when I delivered him his potato salad. This was the evening when he asked me about eggs and, as I read the review, I saw why he had asked. He was fascinated by what the kitchen was doing with the most humble of dishes and ingredients: eggs, potato salad, ice cream cones, "Pop-Tarts." I was thinking about this when Corey walked over. We hadn't said anything to each other yet, although we had both been in the kitchen when Chef Keller arrived with the review. His hands were stuffed deep in his pockets, and I realized that I had seen him only once before without an apron on. I had been walking out of the building after service one night and found him sitting on a ledge smoking a Marlboro.

"You joining us across the street, Corey?" I'd asked, motioning to the Coliseum. Recently it had become quite a scene with the restaurant crowd; we were beginning to get to know the staff of Jean-Georges, Café Gray, V Steakhouse, the Hudson Hotel, and Picholine quite well.

"I think we spend enough time together as it is," he had answered and took a long drag of his cigarette.

But standing there on the night of the review, with his hands shoved awkwardly in his pockets, he looked almost like he might want to join us for a beer. Patrick, Gabriel, and André glanced up from the paper where they had just discovered that we were mentioned in a tiny paragraph on the front page as well.

"Did you see what he said about the veg menu?" Corey asked.

"I was just reading it. I told you he loved that risotto," I said, wondering when this conversation would take its usual turn for the worse.

"Yeah, well, I just wanted to say that I know you were a big part of making that night what it was."

My friends were watching this with amusement, knowing how our exchanges often went. But their eyes could not have grown as wide as mine as Corey leaned across the bar table and gave me a kiss on the cheek. He was out the door before I even recovered.

"Did you see that?" I asked incredulously when I finally moved. They all smiled at me, and André squeezed my hand under the table.

"Chef," he whispered. "*That* was a four-star review."

• A TIP •

Please do not make faces or gagging noises when hearing the specials. Someone else at the table might like to order one of them.

• not in the stars •

ONE MORNING IN early fall, after André left my apartment, I leaned back into my shabby chic thrift store couch—emphasis on the shabby—with a mug of coffee in my hand, and thought about how much I loved my life. Per Se had four stars. I made great money talking about food all day. I worked with passionate, driven future leaders in my field with whom I would spend my time, even if they weren't colleagues. I had a spacious, sunny, nearly one-bedroom apartment for which I paid less than what my friends paid for windowless partitions in dingy lofts. One such friend lived with a balding Web page designer who ate entire supermarket cakes when stoned (a frequent occurrence). He was an improvement on her NYU roommate, who went by Jedi and decorated their room with *Star Wars* action figures. Finally, I had fallen in love with a man with whom I could imagine sharing a life and a spotlight. Just the other day I had caught him staring at me from across the dining room.

"What were you thinking about over there?" I asked him later.

"What our children would look like," he answered.

In short, and in contrast, life was good.

I sighed and took a sip of coffee before rousing my computer. It slept peacefully on a wooden chest, which it shared with a stack of food magazines and the occasional pair of feet. Upon waking, my computer had news for me. André had left his e-mail open.

I scrolled up and down a little, scanning the subject lines of e-mails from managers and the other sommeliers. There were some from Leigh, a couple from his mother, nothing all that surprising. But after a few pages, I noticed that a certain New York cell phone number sent more than its fair share of texts. There it was again. And again. I snapped my computer closed. How would I like it if he were reading my journals? When I opened to the most recent pages of my latest journal, I saw why this should be avoided.

Toast. Toast would be reassuring. My senile old silver toaster required careful observation; if I glanced away for a second, it burst into flames. I had considered replacing it, but it looked great in my 1950s kitchen, next to the vintage fan that I had used for white noise until it too began sparking. It could be anyone. It could be one of the other sommeliers or a persistent wine rep, or a friend he hadn't told me about. My mind wanted to buy that, but the jury of my body, my clammy hands, my hollow heart, the minor chord playing in the pit of my stomach, needed further evidence. Within minutes, my toast was getting cold on the wooden chest while I scrolled through André's entire inbox.

Drinking Margaritas and watching the game.

What are you doing later?

Long day. How are you?

Dinner this week—just us?

Call me when you get a chance.

It seemed that I could open André's e-mail whenever I wanted, without a password. I crawled in when I got home at night, when I woke up in the morning, throughout my days off. I began to think of this mysterious texter as "2040," the last four digits of the phone number—2040, like the minimum vision requirement for a driver's license.

Ironically, things with André were better than ever. He doted on me at work, and he practically moved into my place in Brooklyn when he was off. One day we stopped into a new wine bar that had opened in my neighborhood. It had a real homey feeling to it, in part because of the general store whose entrance it shared. The store sold milk in glass bottles, sausages that hung from the ceiling, and little homemade pies lined up by the register. It was one in a growing number of nostalgic shops and eateries: polka-dotted bakeries, diner cars, rustic hunting lodges, and a surf shack with a sand-covered floor. I had the feeling that there were more out-of-work set designers than I had originally thought, and that all of them were this close to moving back home and planting some sweet peas.

It was early in the evening and the staff was still setting up as we sipped at our rosé and cooled our elbows on the marble tabletop. A little boy drew at a long wooden farm table across the room while the grown-ups discussed which oysters had come in and which cheeses to write up on the chalkboards hanging on each wainscoted wall. Every so often, the little boy held up a drawing for their glowing critique.

"I could own a place like this," André said, surveying the room. I rolled my eyes.

"No, really, I like how simple the room is. Just mismatched tables and stools and a wall of bottles." We looked around, like potential buyers, adding a console here, a meat slicer there.

"I've always thought that would be cool," André said a little while later. "To have kids who grow up in your restaurant."

"Yeah. They stop by after school for a snack. . . ."

"And do their homework while we set up. . . ."

Like all discussions of the future, the conversation began in the abstract and quickly became about us. By the time we left the bar, we had conceived a small business and two children, two to four years apart.

"Would the health department allow a dachshund?"

"French bulldog."

"Whatever."

And still, after conversations like these, I itched for a moment alone to see what 2040 had to say for herself.

The more I read, the more real she became. When I rode the subway, I scrutinized the faces of every attractive woman. Depending on my mood and the book I was reading at the time, she wore go-go boots, pumps, running shoes, or jeweled slippers. I thought of her as I put on my socks. Did hers have holes on the heel like mine? I thought of her when I witnessed, in horror, a renegade roach skitter behind the refrigerator. How often did she mop her floors? I thought of her when I forgot about the water on the stove and ruined yet another pot. When I ran out of things to say or talked too much, when I was too flippant or too serious. And also when I got the hiccups, when my feet cracked, and when I spotted a shadow of a double chin in the mirror. She haunted me in the middle of the night when I became convinced that my teeth were yellowing by the minute. When my mascara smudged, as it did most days. As I obsessed about 2040, I chewed my lower lip until it became pocked. When I drank something particularly tannic, the spots darkened into a deep purple and stayed that way for days. She, I had to believe, had never encountered such a plight. Did she have manicured nails or well-chewed ones like mine? What about pudgy palms? Did she ever order badly or play music long out of style? On the subject of plants, did she understand the fickle temperament of the rosemary, could she coddle a ficus, and tame the vicious spider? Did her hair stick up like the Little Prince in the mornings? She probably never snored. Did he know that?

When André disappeared from view, I wrote even more elaborate fantasies in my head. Their names crowned the guest lists for the newest restaurant openings. They spent André's nights off in secret wine bars or eating takeout in bed. She, of course, wearing spiked heels. On nights we didn't work together, I called as soon as I finished. When he answered, I listened for voices in the background. When he didn't answer, I left a casual message and then took a cab back to Brooklyn, ready to tell the driver to turn back around. As I sat staring at my phone on these long rides, I wondered how I, the queen of independence, had become a slave to another.

We still on for Wednesday?

Not anymore, I thought to myself, before hitting delete with a smug cock of the head. Then I proceeded to panic. What if he looked in his trash? I clicked on it and found 2040's cheery little message crowning the list. What if I just erased the whole trash? No, that might arouse serious suspicion; better to remain calm and hope it would go unnoticed.

At work, when I saw André talking to anyone in the salon, I made it a point to take that route to the bar. One day, he stayed especially long, laughing and chatting with two women seated on the couch closest to the dining room. He stood at the window, his dark suit framed by dark sky and tiny lights. He barely leaned on the window ledge, his arms crossed to reveal the glint of the silver cuff links I liked, the ones shaped like the quill of a pen. A brunette faced me, but her friend sat obscured on the opposite end. The way the back of the couch curved meant that all I could see was blond curls, her hand reaching to squeeze André's arm, and the crossing and uncrossing of tall black boots. That had to be her.

The image of those boots stuck with me for days and I decided that it was time to take a stand. Like a pioneer with a flag, I would claim my man! The irony of my territoriality was not lost on me, but my competitive nature overrode any head-hanging and lesson-learning that might have been appropriate. A few nights later, André and I headed to a little bistro uptown. It was the only place serving croque madame at two o'clock in the morning.

"I don't want you to see anyone else," I blurted out as soon as we sat down.

"Can a brother get a drink first?" André pretended to be annoyed, but he was grinning.

"What's so funny?"

"Leigh was just asking the other day whether we had had this conversation."

"Oh, really."

"Yeah, she says you're late. This usually happens in the first three months."

"You were living with someone for the first three months."

"No need to get competitive." When the waiter cruised by, André ordered a beer for himself, a glass of champagne for me, and a croque madame.

"Did you want anything?"

"No, I'll eat yours."

I waited to continue the conversation until we had sustenance before us. When the food arrived, he took a bite and looked at me, carefully, while he chewed.

"So?" I prodded, getting back to my original question, or to what the question implied.

"So, okay," he said with his mouth full.

"Okay meaning you are not dating anyone else or okay meaning you heard what I said?"

"Okay meaning I'm okay with that."

"No one else?"

"No one else."

That was easy, I thought suspiciously, but only time would tell. Time and 2040.

ELECTION DAY WAS coming up and we scheduled our days off together. André hadn't registered to vote, and I chastised him all the way to the public school down the street where I voted. It was one of those bittersweet late fall days, and after I had cast my hopeful ballot, we wandered around the neighborhood for a while in search of lunch.

"Let's see a movie!"

"What do you want to see?"

"How about *Sideways*?"

As it turned out, this wine-themed movie would shape our destiny. Never again would we serve Merlot. André would have to reorder all of the Pinot Noir, and I would discuss the film at eighty percent of my tables. When I became weary of the topic, I would summon my compassion, telling myself that they ordered the Pinot because they too felt thin-skinned and misunderstood. Because we did not yet know its implications, we enjoyed the film and then headed home to hear the election results on National Public Radio. At first the nation seemed to have regained its sanity. But as more results came in, I began to despair.

"I blame you," I said, glaring at André.

"Whatever. Voting in Texas is just as pointless as voting in New York."

I was too depressed to argue. Eventually, we abandoned all hope and traded NPR for Miles Davis's *Kind of Blue*. I tried to imagine that reality ended at the edges of my couch. It was just André and me and the occasional autumn leaf blowing into the window. We talked for hours, filling each other in on the last twenty-odd years of our lives. And then after a slight pause, André said, "You know, I could have told you I loved you a long time ago."

Such nimble retroaction. He put a Republican Congress to shame.

"Ditto," I responded.

So that was settled. We turned the radio back on just to see if we had missed a miracle. We hadn't. I think it's safe to say you're in love when the apocalypse is near and you couldn't be happier.

BUT THE NEXT day, 2040 announced that she was wearing leather pants.

I was now in a bind. Things with André appeared to be moving along nicely; it was hardly an opportune time to admit to reading his e-mail, let alone calling 2040 from a pay phone on Sixth Avenue.

"Do you really want to get back into another long relationship?" I asked one night, hoping to inspire a confession. "You just ended one. Don't you want to go and sow some oats or test the waters or play the field or something?"

"Chef, I don't have time for that anymore."

When I probed a little more about why things ended with Leigh, he had a vaguely complimentary response.

"It's kind of like I came up for air and found what I didn't know I was looking for."

It was only later, when I was alone, that I started wondering exactly how much air he had taken in. Clearly, I wasn't going to get anything out of him. I'd just have to keep reading. And work toward leather pants.

"Who are you?" André demanded when I refused an ice cream cone a few weeks later. "The woman I fell in love with never said no to ice cream."

"The woman you fell in love with could also stand to lose a few pounds."

"Are you kidding? My prenup is going to have a weight minimum. You lose a pound, I dock you."

Yup, this one was worth fighting for.

• A TIP •

The table is always bigger and quieter on the other side of the restaurant.

• underlings •

SOMETIMES, WHEN I had a moment's pause, I looked out over the dining room at the sculptural desserts, the woven silver breadbaskets, the elaborate napkin fold, and wondered how something as simple as eating had come to this. There's an essay in David Rakoff's second collection called "What Is the Sound of One Hand Shopping?" in which he ridicules the excesses of his adopted society (he was born in Canada). In this particular essay, he skewers the staff, clientele, and earnest, self-important philosophy toward food and farming of a certain restaurant in northern California—which might as well be the French Laundry or Per Se. And he does it in such a way as to implicate anyone who has ever bought imported water or sea salt. Both of which, he observes, we subject to "the kind of scrutiny we used to reserve for choosing an oncologist." I will agree that on the one hand, obsessive attention to dining, ingredients, flavor combinations, and food politics does reflect excessive time and resources in a status-obsessed society. On the other hand, many of our children think chickens have fingers. Is a tasting menu more extreme than artery-clogging, diabetes-inducing fast "food" we barely taste as we're careening down the highway doing eighty?

I often thought of the contrast, and the absurdity, of rattling off the names of the cows that produced the milk used to make the butter while standing in the concrete jungle of New York City. This was the same butter that changed color with seasons I assumed still took place somewhere. I, too, was amused when I heard the man who raised sheep in Pennsylvania explain that the secret to his tender, mild lamb was listening to the animals. Did he not hear them when they were pleading for their lives?

The society to which Mr. Rakoff refers makes a brand out of anything it values. "Heirloom," "sustainable," "organic," and "local" are labels that have become just another form of branding in a label-obsessed society, complete with a low-end line at Wal-Mart. As evidence of this trend, the Per Se menu reads like a fashion magazine, only instead of the cut, color, and designer, we had the cut, color, and farmer. Potatoes weren't potatoes, they were pureed purple marble potatoes from Mr. McGregor's garden. Cavendish Farms quail, Snake River Farms beef, Four Story Hills veal, Hallow Farms rabbit, Thumbelina carrots, Pink Lady apples, and wild arugula were similarly gussied.

But when it comes to food, I'm as label-conscious as my mall-going girlfriends across the river. When I lovingly prepare breakfast for my future children, I'd at least like to know that I served them Monsanto-engineered cornflakes with rBGH-infused milk, diazinon-sprayed strawberries, and irradiated bananas. That way, I know who to thank for their food allergies, prepubescent breasts, autism, and leukemia. I have to believe that the more curious we become about our food, the better off we'll be.

In the meantime, while waiting for global change, I decided that I wanted to meet some of the restaurant's purveyors so that I wouldn't feel like such a fake at the table, so that I would actually understand where the food came from, who raised it, and why it was worth so very much. There was plenty to choose from, but my first thought was visiting the heirloom ducks we started to see on the menu in the fall. When I asked Corey for a contact number, he rolled his eyes.

"It's not a petting zoo, you know."

My other choices included a farm that raised milk-fed chickens (from powder, not a bottle), a family (whom I'd served and loved) who grew oysters near Cape Cod, an organic farm out on Long Island run by a chef, and a rabbi who foraged for watercress and ramps upstate. One project I found particularly interesting was a special beer and cheese pairing arranged with a dairy in Vermont. The dairy, Jasper Hill Farm, was run by two brothers new to the cheese-making field. The Per Se pairing consisted of a beer brewed by a friend of theirs and the pungent Winnemere, a raw cow's milk cheese bound in spruce bark and washed with the same beer. The beer was called Agatha, which is, I believe, where the confusion began.

Somehow, in the proverbial game of telephone, the information became slightly distorted and the staff understood the cheese to have been made from the milk of a single cow by the name of Agatha. A single-cow cheese. I had heard of single-bean coffee and chocolate, but never of a single-cow cheese. What was next? Single-nest eggs? Single-stalk brussels sprouts? One night during Winnemere season, André left work shaking his head.

"Chef, I have a story for you. But first I need to get out of this suit. And then I need a drink."

Apparently, a VIP from the food sector had been scheduled to come in for dinner and the kitchen wanted him to try the Agatha/Winnemere pairing. The restaurant had just run out of the beer, so André sent a coffee server down to the wine storage facility in Chelsea to pick up a six-pack. This was how important this table was. They enjoyed champagne and extra canapés and the famous host seemed to be a jovial sort, but when it came to the cheese course, the meal went sour.

"At first I thought he was just joking when he started flipping out, so I played along," André told me. "But he refused to eat the cheese. He just kept shaking his head and saying 'Absurd!'"

Eventually the gentlemen's guests, André, and the captain realized that the guy was truly incensed by the concept of a single-cow cheese. They quickly arranged a different cheese-and-wine pairing. But André couldn't wrap his head around it. What had he been so upset about?

Always a sucker for scandal, I decided that I wanted to meet Agatha and see if I could track down the VIP. Meanwhile, I would get out of the city for a weekend and gorge myself on cheese. As a lover of all cheese, the stinkier the better, I have been excited, and a little perplexed, by the boom in domestic artisanal production in the last ten years. There are now luscious examples to be found in Louisiana, Texas, and the great cheese state of Connecticut. Places like Vermont that have always been known for dairy are teeming with small producers.

Jasper Hill Farm is located in Greensboro, Vermont, in the heart of the Northeast Kingdom. When their cheese was on the menu at Per Se, this information was posted in the breezeway, along with a taste profile, and everyone found the name "Northeast Kingdom" to be terribly amusing. If only they knew the irony—that the majestic name actually described one of the poorest, most untamed parts of Vermont. The kind of place where school might as well be canceled on the first day of hunting season. André and I flew up on the last flight out of JFK one Saturday night after he got out of work. We flew into Burlington, the largest city in Vermont, at about forty thousand, where my mother had recently bought a little house. I'll leave the back door open, she told me over the phone.

The next morning we got up early and drove our rental car out to the farm. Thrifty car rental gave us a PT Cruiser, a car I always found dippy. I prepared André to be ridiculed by my brother, who is very selective when it comes to certain brands and lifestyle choices. He disdains, for example, most small dogs and Jet Skis. Sam has a deal with his two best friends from college that if any of them ever gets a minivan, the other two have the right to bump him off with no warning. So, in our little PT Cruiser, André and I sped past the Ben & Jerry's factory in Waterbury and on through Mercedes-infested Stowe. We traded ski condos for dilapidated farmhouses and trailers, pink triangles for yellow ribbons. After an hour or so, we stopped trailing Subarus with bumper stickers like "Compost Happens" and "Breast-feeding: Anytime, Anywhere" and other random acts of crunchy kindness. A call-in radio show devoted entirely to yard sale announcements took a station break to advertise an outdoor event called "Grills Gone Wild." Cows manicured a pasture of abandoned farm equipment, which stood stoic and rusting like a sculpture garden.

When I called for directions, Mateo, one of the two brothers who runs the farm, told me to turn right at the light. Which light? There was only one. We kept following the directions, involving Laundromats and police stations, but no street names, until the road became dirt and the houses farther and farther apart. Finally, we pulled into the driveway and down a slight hill to a barn attached to a house that looked like it was evolving slowly. It was a hot day and the two dogs who came to greet us were dusty from rolling in the cool earth in the shade of the barn.

Mateo and Andy Kehler bought the farm in 1998, never intending to make cheese. They had grown up in South America, but wanted to move to the Northeast Kingdom, where their mother's family was from. Much of the family still lives in the area; during our visit, one cousin stopped by and a family friend came in from one of the fields where he had been working. Determined to settle there, the two brothers had a few ideas about how they would make a living. Before attempting cheese, they even contemplated making tofu, although Andy told us they only ever made it in their own kitchen on a very small scale.

Not all cheese-makers allow visitors, for fear of disturbing the fragile environment. But not all cheese-makers play Grateful Dead in their barn, either. We were instructed to take off our own shoes, however, and select a pair of rubber clogs from a pile. We each put on a hairnet (even bald André) and washed our hands at the sink by the door with the casual protraction of surgeons. To our right as we walked in was a big stainless-steel vat attached to a line that runs from the barn. When Andy milks the cows in the morning, it's in the vat within minutes. Unlike many cheese-making facilities that have to have the milk delivered to them, Jasper Hill milk never waits more than twenty-four hours before it becomes cheese. Andy walked us through the whole process, from separating the whey to salting, shaping, and aging.

After we had gotten to know one another a little, André inquired after Agatha. Agatha, as it turned out, was dead. And they produced no such thing as a single-cow cheese.

"I suppose we could," Andy mused, "but it would be a real pain."

Agatha was their first cow that birthed. She had been ahead of schedule, before the cheese-making facility had been completed, and Andy had to milk her by hand. The beer had been named for her, but that was the extent of her involvement. So much for controversy.

Andy explained that they went through eight hundred pounds of salt every six weeks. Which made me think of my friend David Rakoff.

"What kind?" I asked him.

"Sea salt," he informed me and then went on to describe how hard it was to find a salt with no additives. I probed a little, mockingly referring to the excessive array of overpriced salts now on the market. Andy couldn't disagree more.

"The more we have to choose from, the better," he said.

Now that I think about it, I realize that I asked the question with a dash of overprivileged, consumer guilt. What had I been expecting, that he would look at me blankly as if he had never heard of anything but iodized supermarket brands? No indeed; I had met a salt connoisseur here in the Northeast Kingdom.

In 1970 Greensboro, Vermont, had thirty-three dairy farms. In 2006 there were nine. Andy thought that this year, with the increase in fuel and transportation costs, would be especially tough. Just two days earlier, the town's largest dairy farmer had approached them about selling his milk to Jasper Hill. This is not something they are necessarily interested in, because of the risks of possible contamination. But they would consider building a cheese-making facility on other farms.

In a time where local farmers find they can no longer survive selling the products they have relied on, creating a reverse AOC might be their only hope. In Europe, certain regional products, such as prosciutto di parma or balsamic vinegar from Modena, are only allowed to be made in those regions. In exchange for following certain rules and traditions, these local producers maintain a protected monopoly over certain coveted ingredients. Mateo and Andy, if they played their cards right, could establish something like this with their cheeses and save a dying industry.

It is not an easy time for farmers, and more and more we hear the leaders in food and agriculture industries calling for action on a local level. Andy and Mateo could buy organic feed from Canada and eat up tons of fuel transporting it. Or they could buy hay from the farmer down the road and help keep him afloat. Of course, they would love to be organic, but they also believe that if we are going to have any control over our food supply, we need to keep it close to home.

The brothers think a lot about their neighbors. When we went downstairs to the cool concrete aging facility, we saw cheeses from all over the state. A lot of time and care goes into aging cheese. It has to be turned so it ripens evenly; patted, so the mold doesn't build into an overthick rind; pricked, so the mold can penetrate; and worried over, because cheeses, much like children, pets, and plants, need to be coddled. In France, the title of such an artist is *affineur*. Jasper Hill provides this time-consuming service for large cheese-makers such as Cabot, whose rounds take up a wall in the basement cave, and smaller producers who lack the temperature and humidity-controlled space. We saw sheep's milk cheeses from another neighbor, a few precious rounds from the oldest creamery in the country, down in Crowley, Vermont. And Jasper Hill's own cheeses, of course.

The fluffy white mold growing on the Constant Bliss made

the little cheeses look like iced cakes from a distance and baby chicks up close. There were planks and planks of their two blues, Bayley Hazen and Bartlett Blue. At the far end of the wall lurked the cheddarlike Aspenhurst. These large rounds take up to eighteen months to age. The farm produces very few at the moment because with such slow turnover, they aren't cost-effective. Much of the work on those is done around the beginning of the year, or as Andy called it, "resolution season."

"Let's go see the cows," he suggested after we had seen the operation.

On the way down the hill, he pointed out the site of a new barn that they had been working on until it blew over. They had put up three sides and the roof when an eighty-mile-per-hour wind came along and, as he put it, turned it into a sail. Andy, who once worked as a contractor, had been happy to build it the first time around. But not twice. He unplugged the electric fence and lowered it so we could climb over. The grass was thick and green and barely revealed the thick pies that lurked every few feet.

"Mmmmmmooo," Andy called in a low voice.

They cows answered in unison.

When they are both around, Mateo runs the cheese end and Andy takes care of the animals. Although they have their specialties, the brothers have made sure they each know every aspect of the operation so that they have the flexibility to go on vacation, to food shows, and the like.

Jasper Hill uses Ayrshire cows because of the natural homogenization of the milk. It is actually closer to goat milk than, say, the milk of Jerseys. If you leave Jersey milk out, you will soon find that a thick layer of fat rises—making it ideal for butter-making. But if you want a rich cheese milk that will ripen quickly, you want something more homogenized. Ayr-shires, like the French Normandes and Montbeliard, do just this. They are rust and cream-colored, some mostly cream with red freckles, some mostly red.

A gregarious heifer named Gizmo sidled over and began to drool on my bare toe. This was when it really hit me. The last time I talked this much about cows, I was standing in a suit and tie in a high-rise looking out over Fifty-ninth Street. Now, a wide, rough tongue was attempting to lick my belly. By attempting, I mean that she was butting her bony fore-head against me and soaking my T-shirt, but not quite man-aging to lift it. I was flattered and scratched the tuft of hair between her long-lashed eyes. André, I noticed, was keeping his distance. Every so often the cows would have a tussle over a particularly tasty clump of grass and there would be a mass shuffling. André quickly backed away.

"Was someone a little scared of the cows?" I teased him on the way back up the hill.

"Anyways. I like having ten toes." Andy had informed us that his herd weighed in the 900- to 1,100-pound range.

The cows had no particular interest in André, either. They had more than their fair share of visitors. Elementary schools trooped through, as did the farmers who had retired to a home nearby. They'd have you know that they had none of these newfangled machines—they milked their herds by hand.

After we had seen the cows, Andy wanted to show us his new pigs. This was an experiment, he explained. In what? Well, air-dried hams, among other things. But when he hopped in the pen and started chasing them around, I wondered whether they would even see a knife. The man was literally frolicking. When I asked Andy about his models, he told me about a man in Virginia who had a large operation involving cows, pigs, and chickens. The pigs ate the whey from the cheese, and the chickens ate the insects from the cow pastures. This might not work with a small farm like Jasper Hill, but they were on their way. The eight pigs, Humpty, Dumpty, Piggly, Wiggly, Eeny, Meeny, Miney, and Mo, already ate the whey, and Andy was considering chickens.

When we got back to the main barn and our dippy ride, we dug out the bottle of Laurent Perrier 1996 champagne we had brought thinking it would go well with the Constant Bliss. In exchange, Andy let us pick out a little cheese for dinner. On went the clogs again and down we trooped into the cave. We chose Constant Bliss and Winnemere, which Andy packed up on ice for the ride.

On the drive to my brother's house, where breast-feeding does indeed happen anytime and anywhere, we talked about the visit. It was like visiting vineyards, André said. Here you have this product that has the reputation of being pretentious, with French names and useless dates, and it is easy to forget that it is made by someone with mud on his boots.

When we got to Sam's house, there was a minivan parked out front. Apparently his truck had died, and he had been forced to borrow a car from a friend. The perfect opportunity to tease my brother unmercifully, it was a senseless act of beauty.

DESPITE ITS HUMBLE origins, artisanal cheese is considered by most consumers to be a luxury product. But what really defines luxury? And when has something gone too far? For that VIP who was misinformed about the single-cow cheese, a line had been crossed between luxury and excess. But he might very well have a $14,000 refrigerator at home and be perfectly comfortable with that.

Per Se is expensive, there is no way around it. But so are paintings and plane tickets and evenings at the theater. Friends often explained, apologetically, that they would love to eat at Per Se, but they just couldn't afford to. If that were true, I would have understood. I'm not discounting true poverty. But the same people who balked at the price of the tasting menu regularly spent a similar sum on concert tickets, gadgets, software, or shoes they didn't really need. People expect to pay for art and travel, but when faced with three-digit menu prices, they react as if it were some perverse compulsion.

Not everyone who came to Per Se was a millionaire. At one table, a line cook and his date blew months of savings on a meal and a half bottle of our least expensive Sancerre. One table over, two brothers in the finance business spent their usual $20,000 on a few bottles and drank only half. If they were merely hungry, they would have grabbed a slice; instead, they paid for the memory, the communion, the relaxation, and the shared experience.

I discovered early on that André and I had a very similar approach to spending. Neither of us had a car. We did not own real estate. We didn't spend much on clothes. We rarely went to the theater or concerts. We didn't buy art or expensive furniture or large televisions or sound systems. We spent money on two things: food and something we soon named "everyday luxury." Under this heading fell things like eight-dollar toothpaste. Yes, toothpaste can be had for a quarter of that, but we decided that if it increased our love of life at least twice a day, it was worth it. The softest underwear. Good coffee, butter, jam, and mustard. Cabs. Flowers. Slab bacon. Triple-ply toilet paper. Big, fluffy towels and bathrobes. Magazine subscriptions. Cuff links and silver bracelets. Wine. Day trips. Of course, everyday luxury is in the eye of the beholder. For some people, it might be boxed cereal, a dye job, or day care. For others, it might be a private jet or a Calder mobile.

I understand the risk involved. If I'm not careful, I will end up being part of what David Rakoff calls an "army of multiply chemically sensitive, high-maintenance princesses trying to make our way through a world of irksome peas." The kind of person who categorically refuses to drink tap water. I have a few good friends who have promised to bump me off with no warning if this becomes the case.

It's all a roundabout way of saying that I don't want anyone reading this to feel guilty about paying for good food. Or reading about people paying for good food. Gas-guzzling cars and blood diamonds, yes. Organic, heirloom, sustainable, local, real food, no. Now go out and buy some cheese.

• A TIP •

Most white wine should be served at about 55 degrees and red wine at 67 degrees. We are happy to further chill a white or decant the red to bring up the temperature, but please do not ask us to microwave your wine.

• i can hear you •

I BEGAN HYPOTHESIZING ABOUT universal shame one day at Baby Girl's Bubbles & Cleaners. I was doing my laundry after someone broke the handle off the washing machine. Unlike washing clothes at home, where wet laundry happily hangs out in the machine for hours before it starts to smell, in a Laundromat, one is held hostage, staring through the porthole of the dryer as that one last sweatshirt goes around and around. I hold a certain plush white towel responsible for the trauma I experienced when a show titled *I Love You—How Could You Sleep with My Mom?* came on to a television hanging from the ceiling. I have no defense mechanisms when it comes to television, probably from years of living without one. I become a slave to the blue light, and when I finally come to, I ruminate for days over what I have seen.

At first I was horrified that people would *choose* to reveal the pale, fragile underbelly of their souls to the millions of viewers pointing and laughing in living rooms and Laundromats across the country. The jilted daughters on the show yelled and cried and threatened to call off their engagements. The audience booed and cheered. I watched in horror and recounted the scene for André later in full detail—quotes and all.

"That show really got to you?"

"Chef, I have never seen anything like it. It was like . . ."

"A three-ring circus in a trailer park?"

"Exactly!"

Some of us wear habits and some of us paint beach scenes on our nails, but I think all of us have a story we would prefer not to share. This goes for the Laundromat, for me, and especially for restaurant dining rooms.

AT SIX O'CLOCK, two elderly couples settle in on table twenty-one to celebrate the men's shared eightieth birthdays. They have already had martinis and Macallan 12 in the salon and taken turns visiting the bathroom for mysteriously long periods, which seemed not to faze their spouses. Upon sitting, the gentleman at position four tucks his napkin behind his yellow bowtie with a cheer endearing to anyone watching, except perhaps his wife who doesn't mind it at home, but hoped that perhaps tonight he would place it on his lap like a civilized person. Having been married more than fifty years, she is bored by her husband, even before she wakes in the morning. This is not to say that she doesn't love him, it is just that there comes a time when the person you love ceases to be entertaining—just like the face in the mirror that has lost its intrigue. She turns toward the woman next to her, whose mate has placed his napkin politely over his lap, for which she loves him slightly more at this moment, but has already ordered his third scotch and now turns his attention to the wine list. The women talk to each other for the duration of the meal, pausing every so often to make sure their husbands are still breathing. By dessert, both men are not only breathing, they are snoring heavily as their heads droop dangerously close to their glasses of Madeira.

THE GENTLEMAN ON table twenty-three plans to propose and has arranged for us to deliver a Fabergé egg at the end of their meal. Proposals are nerve-racking for everyone involved. While terrified lovers contemplate eternity in sickness, poverty, death, or worse, equally anxious servers imagine ruining what might be the high point of these people's lives together, before the bankruptcy, the Botox, and his affair with the life coach.

We seat them in one of two private banquettes with a view of the restaurant and the park so that, if all goes well, they can snuggle close and debate hyphenation. She seems a little jumpy, and I wonder if someone has tipped her off or whether she just has a feeling about this one. We clear the table after the cheese course, leaving only the candle and two glasses of champagne. The maître d' arrives with a wooden box (the humidor we usually use for truffles) on a silver tray and bows to the lady with great ceremony.

"Oh!" she gasps, placing her ringless hand on her heart and gazing at her intended with dewy eyes before she reaches for the egg. The maître d' closes the truffle box and steps away from the table, keeping close enough to witness the moment.

It is all we can do to feign calm when she opens the egg and there is not a ring in sight. She begins to cry. Her fiancé instructs her as to the egg's value (which we Googled on the computer in the kitchen and determined to be somewhere between $500 and $5.5 million) and she pretends to be moved, but I know that she is heartbroken.

He eats his sorbet and dessert with gusto while she prods at hers with her spoon, crestfallen. When he finally pulls the ring from his pocket, her joy is more like a worn relief. I imagine she will tell her girlfriends how clever his elaborate and extravagant proposal had been. But I wonder whether she will always think of how small and alone she felt when she opened the egg and realized that he would never know how to read her heart. Perhaps she will think of it as the first time she ignored the truth.

ALTHOUGH HIS PARTY is incomplete, the silver-haired gentleman in tweed has been seated at a prominent table. He drinks a gin and tonic with lime (G&T as he and his wife call it when they take their places in their Fifth Avenue suite at five o'clock on the dot, he in an armchair with the *Journal*, she on the love seat with the dog). From the looks of him, I predict an overly blond woman in a short-skirted suit of an obscene hue.

She arrives eventually, just as I imagined, in a salmon pink suit, handbag, and matching shoes, with jarringly lifted eyes that appear perpetually alarmed, and crispy hair the color of a winter dog run. What I did not predict was that she would request a third chair for her dog. This is not a toy poodle or shih tzu, nor is it a taxidermist's resurrection; it is an actual stuffed doggish animal, although more reminiscent of Alf. The initial challenge is composure, followed by an attempt at graciousness. But in the end, it is all we can do to fend off free drinks sent to the dog from diners around the room who pretend to see nothing out of the ordinary when we turn toward them to glare. At the end of the meal, she takes out her lip

gloss, the kind applied with a squishy-tipped wand, and pro-
ceeds to search for the exact location of her inflated lips, stab-
bing the wand to either side, while thrusting them forward
like a snowplow.

THE COUPLE SITTING on table eight seems to me the picture of the American family. He is a broker with a soft chin
who commutes from Greenwich; she is a dumpling of a woman
whom I can see hanging clothes on a line while a pie cools in
the window. They opt, with my prodding, for the chef's tasting menu and settle into their meal with grateful ease. As we
begin to chat, I learn that they recently moved to the area
with a new baby and that this is their first dinner out together
since she was born. They are having a hard time adjusting to
the pace of New York (even if filtered by the commute) after
having lived in both Washington, D.C., and Denver. She misses
the outdoors, calling herself more liberal than her suburban
neighbors. The pace of Wall Street exhausts him.

All of my tables are seated within minutes of one another,
which means that just as I have the food and wine order from
one table, another arrives. For this reason, I only have a chance
to stop by table eight a few times during their meal to top off
their wine and spiel a dish or two.

By the time it comes to their dessert, my other tables are
under way and I have some time to chat. The dessert today is
the Snickers Bar, a deconstructed version of the classic, with a
chocolate Sacher cake, salted caramel, nougat ice cream, and
peanut milk gelée. The gentleman takes one bite and closes his
eyes in ecstasy.

"This is better than pot," he says definitively to his wife,
who nods in agreement.

There have been times when a seemingly conservative guest has surprised me with a quote from the movie *Airplane*, a Simpsons reference, or leftist politics, but this one leaves me gaping. The fine-dining waiter in me suspects that I should just nod and smile and pour a little more water, but the child of hippie parents from Vermont prevails. I decide to venture gingerly into the topic. Isn't it my job to make the guest feel comfortable?

"Do you indulge?" I ask politely.

"Two or three times a week," he answers, beaming at his wife, whose rosy cheeks dimple in response.

You just never know about people, I think. This is the suit I make fun of on Madison Avenue, with his *Wall Street Journal* tucked under his arm, filing in with the other suits to a Smith & Wollensky steak house with their cigar-smoking bosses. But little do I know that he is probably just jonesing for a rib-eye after having smoked a blunt before getting on Metro North. I am filled with newfound appreciation for this man and determined to make him feel comfortable with having shared such intimate details.

"That's great!" I assure him. "I don't smoke much myself, but I feel like it's always been part of my culture. I grew up with my mother growing it beside the driveway, many of my friends are regular smokers. . . ."

As I say this, I notice his face clouding in confusion. He looks over at his wife and then back at me and, for a moment, I think he is just surprised to have found a kindred spirit.

"I said 'pie.'"

SOMETIMES DRUGS ARE the only explanation. Like on Easter when a couple wanders in, attempting to balance eggs on their heads. They are staying in rooms at the Mandarin Hotel upstairs, to which they are sent to change out of their white denim and put on more formal attire. Apparently, they just flew in from Miami on their private jet. They are in town to buy hotels and were hoping to meet with their broker as they eat. Do we mind if a guest joins them for drinks at the table? The poor man is left alone on table six between every course, sipping calmly at his single-malt scotch, while they powder their noses in the bathroom.

THE MAN SITTING on table two looks like a cross between Frederick Douglass and James Brown. I am excited to have someone who is not white, and not a banker, tourist, or underemployed philanthropist. He announces that he will drink Cuba Libres all night and I recognize a familiar lilt to his words. When I ask him what type of rum he prefers, I ask to confirm my suspicion and feel victorious when he tells me that he prefers Barbancourt. I throw a victorious look over my shoulder at André, who is waiting for me to get out of the way so he can approach the table about wine. I have been lobbying for Barbancourt since we opened, partly because it is the best rum on the planet and partly because I lived in Haiti briefly as a child and want to do all I can to support the country and its limping economy.

"Ki gen ou vle? Cinqe etoile ou trois?" Of course, my asking what kind of Barbancourt he drinks is misleading as we don't carry any at all, but he is too astounded to notice, after discovering a white kreyol speaker at a restaurant where the average check for a table of four is just under the per capita yearly income of his countrymen.

Both his three dining companions and my three other tables suffer for the rest of the evening, because we take every opportunity to discuss everything from Haitian politics to goat purveyors. After he orders, he calls me over to request some peppers. We reminisce about picklies, the pickled hot pepper condiment that Haitians serve with fried plantains.

The Per Se kitchen can accommodate any allergy, make gluten-free bread, run out to the deli around the corner to buy Red Bull on request, and whip up chicken noodle soup for a sniffling guest who couldn't taste his meal. But when I go to J.B. to request "pepper service on table two," he is not amused. Luckily, one of the sous chefs saw some Scotch bonnets come in that morning and offers to grab a few. Next thing I know, a vested runner strides purposefully from the kitchen with an array of chili options arranged in ceramic bowls on a silver tray. There is sriracha sauce, kept for family meal on taco day, and a selection of diced peppers. The maître d' wanders over to see what is going on; the runner who presented the tray stays to watch the response. André, my backserver, and I all remain close as well. As he takes the sriracha and dumps it right onto the Russian sevruga caviar in his Oysters and Pearls, I have to avert my eyes.

When I return to the kitchen to ask for a second service, the chef looks puzzled.

"But he has only had one course." Then he gasps. "He *didn't* put hot sauce in his Oysters and Pearls."

The first thing you learn as a waiter is when to get the hell out of the kitchen.

IT MIGHT COME as a surprise to know that Per Se has regulars, like any restaurant. Some go through the sixty-day reservation system; some spend $20,000 on their first visit and hop the line in the future. I went to watch one of my favorite regulars perform in the *Nutcracker* at Lincoln Center, another I met for lunch, and with some I corresponded via e-mail. Although I could tell a story about each of these guests, I will respect their anonymity—except in one case. I feel comfortable telling her story because she is not only one of the most fascinating people I have ever met, but because she will not be bothered in the slightest to know that she is being talked about. In fact, I think she assumes this to be the case.

"Eve" is in her midtwenties and claims to have been engaged nineteen times. She often dines with her partner (I did not ask whether he was number nineteen, a future number twenty, or will remain unnumbered), an Englishman with the understated and befuddled look of a marriageable vicar out of a Trollope novel. Just as often she entertains friends, dashing single gentlemen, or dines alone. Eve is one of the few guests who have had both lunch and dinner at the restaurant on the same day. She is quite petite, with porcelain skin and almond-colored eyes that match her long hair, which is usually pulled back. She is always curiously dressed—in large hat sculptures, transparent sheaths, or sarilike pantsuits. When the maître d' announces that she will be dining at the restaurant, someone always mumbles the reminder maxim: no peppers, no fennel, no bra.

If her gentleman friend belongs to Trollope, Eve belongs to Fitzgerald. She seems often to have just returned from a mysterious destination where she has been "resting" after a bit of "exhaustion." Once she vaguely referred to a surgery. On occasion, "in dire need of a nap," she asked to have a room booked for her at the Mandarin or the Essex House.

Whether ill, recovering, or exhausted, Eve has a story that will make even the most seasoned among us blush. Sixty-eight out of sixty-nine times it will involve some sort of sordid sexual behavior.

One day Eve enjoys a long lunch on table two with two young gentlemen. They are the last in the dining room, and I am alone keeping watch while the rest of the staff enjoys the family meal of fish and chips, which, if I recall correctly, was a parting gift from an English cook on his last day. I stand by the door, waiting with boxes of chocolates, trying to encourage them to depart so that we can reset the table before the first dinner guests arrive. On her way out, Eve puts her hand on my arm and leans close.

"My friend has just told me the most incredible thing. Don't be shocked."

I brace myself.

"Apparently the new thing is to shit in a condom, freeze it, and use it as a dildo!"

And with that she floats away, leaving me with my hand clapped over my mouth and my eyes wide. When I am sure she is quite gone, I sprint to the sommelier station. André stands with the rest of the wine team, with greasy fingers and tartar sauce in the corner of his mouth.

"Get this," I begin.

WE REMOVE THE chair from position three on table two to make room for the wheelchair. A short man, who appears to be in his seventies, wheels a woman of similar age as close as he can get her to the table. He adjusts her legs, props her up a little, and places her napkin so that it rests over her breasts and lap. After making her comfortable, he pulls his own chair closer to her, away from the window and the view of the park in the early-evening light. When I approach with menus,

I look to him for direction, but she tells me exactly how she wants me to prop the menu so that she can read it.

"Rabbit!" she exclaims when she spots the chef's tasting menu. "I love rabbit!"

I am shy around handicapped people. I am self-conscious, for example, with someone who reads lips. Am I overannunciating? Should I pause and wait for eye contact or would that be insulting? If at all possible, I will not help a blind person across the street—not because I don't care, but because I'm sure there's some right way to do it that I don't know. Even a wandering eye flusters me.

This is one reason why, when the maître d' goes through the reservations for the evening, I find myself on edge. Proposals and allergies bring their own anxiety because of the disastrous implications of a blunder. Celebrities and press make me tense. Even children cause me to overthink my service as I try to be kid-friendly without being belittling or excessively animated. The forewarning of a wheelchair causes jitters of equal magnitude. Of course, what I always forget is that these guests spend their entire lives dealing with people like me and are prepared to tell me exactly what to do.

She orders her rabbit and he selects from the five-course menu. They do not order wine, but André remains in my station anyway. Together we watch as the husband carefully feeds her the entire tasting menu.

"Now that is how you love someone," André says quietly.

THE AVERAGE GUEST spends about three hours at Per Se, during which time she allows herself a little more than usual of everything: carbs, cleavage, calories, and certainly, more cocktails. This may account for the fact that more people throw up in the dining room of Per Se than your average college bar. Once, a woman on the upper level leaned over the balcony while staggering down the stairs and vomited on a table below. But it is a testament to the stamina of some that they head to the bathroom, clean themselves up, and proceed with their meal.

THE WOMAN ON table six is still here. Her guest has even paid their bill and left. Assuming she will eventually leave as well, I decide to polish a few trays and wait it out. Ten minutes later, when I peek around the corner into my otherwise empty station, she is craning her neck and scanning the dining room. I'm afraid I know who she is looking for.

On our first night together, she informed me that the captain who took care of her on a previous visit had been pretentious and that, so far, she liked me much better. Thrilling, I thought. She called ahead to request me before each of her next few visits, and I soon had her particularities down. She preferred to drink from the most expensive hand-blown glasses, sample our most aggressive cheeses, but most of all, she liked to be out-Diva'd.

"She's fabulous," she would tell her guests with a grand gesture toward me, as if recommending a house specialty. Her guests looked at me skeptically, waiting for me to be fabulous.

Once, the maître d' ignored her request and seated her upstairs when I was working below. When she demanded to be moved, he lied and told her that I was in great demand and the other tables had requested me first. The staff had a big laugh at that one.

"I see I will have to be much more clear the next time I

make a reservation," she said in a huff. Every time I looked up, she was watching me.

Tonight she seemed intent on learning as much about my life as possible.

"You never have time to talk anymore," she whined when I tried to extricate myself. I reluctantly answered a few questions about my life, my neighborhood, my possible future plans, my more immediate plans for a snack after work. She was riveted. While I agreed that burgers and beers at the Corner Bistro were just what I needed after ten hours of spoiling others, it was far from riveting.

"No, you don't understand," she said tragically, "you're free." I almost expected her to put her thin, pale hand to her head and sigh as she detailed her personal prison, the firm hours, the bills, the monotonous client dinners. She certainly made it sound dismal, but how bad could a life be that involved extra cheese courses and hand-blown stemware?

Now she sits, one hand guarding her fishbowl of a glass, the other hand drumming its fingers impatiently. That's it, I think, my day is too long to play this game. After her leisurely tasting menu, she has been here for a good four hours and I feel completely justified in leaving.

I walk confidently over to her table, inform her of my decision, and point out the captain who will help her if there is anything else she needs. He waves and she shoots him a look of disgust.

"But I thought we were going out for burgers." Her whine and pout are a perfect match.

AFTER SPENDING AT least one evening with each of these fascinating characters, I became weary of discussing which celebrities I encountered. All of them, I would respond before changing the subject. But the truth was, I did meet my share of the rich and famous and noticed a few patterns.

- On the whole, celebrities seem to have a large cranium—literally big heads. I bet if you took an average, celebrity heads would prove larger than those belonging to the rest of us. It could be argued that their bodies tend to be smaller, but even the bigger ones have big heads. I wonder if it is one of those survival-of-the-fittest things—like tall presidents and women with big breasts.
- Celebrities are usually the last in their party to show up. Perhaps this is another survival tactic, as food tasters once were for royalty. Or maybe being fashionably late really does get you somewhere in life.
- Celebrities love to be allergic to things. Either that or they are so bored by good food that they have to spice it up by asking for an all-mushroom tasting menu (famous news anchor) or being allergic to any or all of the following: nuts, fish with scales, fish without scales, shellfish, all fish, wheat, dairy, sugar, chocolate, egg yolks, duck eggs, onions, garlic, pineapple, mango, peppers, fennel, and the list goes on. As a server, it is hard to know what to take seriously. Will she really go into anaphylactic shock if she eats sprouts or an Indian spice? Will she keel over from a little butter in her sauce? Obviously, the kitchen takes allergies seriously, but if a professed vegetarian just ordered foie gras, a little chicken stock will not kill her.

I have mentioned the cute list before; veal, rabbit, venison, and lamb tend to inspire the quivering lip.

"I can't eat Thumper," they tell me with puppy-dog eyes, "or Bambi, either."

How about Daffy? I always want to ask. What about Bessie the cow or Sammy the salmon? Bernard the brussels sprout—he's cute!

- Celebrities are not as attractive in person. But they usually have the best hair, skin, and shoes in the room.
- Celebrities love to talk about other celebrities, but only by their first names—just to keep you guessing. Which Bobby could it be? De Niro? Duval? Redford? Reiner? Billy Bob?
- If there are multiple celebrities in the same room, the rules state that they must get up and speak to one another. At this point, they do their secret handshake and exchange the code word. (This is done almost imperceptibly, which is why you probably have never noticed.) If they are actors, they will both get up and greet each other in the center of the dining room. If they are politicians, the one who plans to lobby, bribe, or slander the other makes the move. If they are in comedy or music, any of the above may be done, but only when leaning on something in the flow of traffic or draping an arm in such a way as to make it impossible for a plate or bottle to come between them. Ballet dancers are required to double kiss; anyone in the news must say the other person's name at least twice during the exchange; and

socialites and old money are allowed to skip all
pleasantries until they are on their way out, at
which point they follow a script along the lines
of: "Oh, hello, (insert first name, last name, title,
"darling," or "guy" here)! I didn't even *see* you!"
Now a complimentary comment is required:
"Doesn't that look deli*s*h!" "That dress is fabulous!"
(Shortening to fab is not usually well received—
nor is calling someone "guy" for that matter.)
"Good game last weekend!" Etc.

We may not have dined together at Per Se and we certainly
weren't celebrities, but André and I had the universal shame
thing down. We didn't need a daytime talk show to reveal the
fragile underbellies of our souls, though our triangulation, de-
ceit, and penchant for drama might have landed us a spot if we
had been so inclined.

It was New Year's and we were taking our first vacation.
The restaurant would close for a week, and most of our colleagues had bought tickets to places like Thailand, Italy, and
Sweden months before. By the time André and I got around
to planning our trip, the prices had gone through the roof.
Finally, a friend offered her place on the beach in Puerto Rico
and we found a cheap flight on JetBlue. It didn't matter where
we went, really; we just needed a break.

The other major event was that Leigh had decided to leave
New York. I imagine that living in a small studio with one's
ex, in a city one hates, while working an uninspiring and low-
paying job provided a pretty miserable existence. When we got
back from vacation, she would be gone. I had a hard time hiding my relief from André.

We did practically nothing in Puerto Rico. We shared papaya in the mornings and thick, dark coffee. During the day, we sat on the beach and took walks without a destination. In the evenings after dinner, we drank Spanish wine and lounged in the hammock. It was perfect.

"To surviving the year," I said, holding up my glass.

"I'll drink to that," André responded.

I lay in the hammock while André sat at a little table in the courtyard, smoking a cigarette. I was a bad influence. I smoked one solitary cigarette a day, usually after work or in my window in Brooklyn. Now André, the nonsmoker, was racing through the pack and, apparently, relishing the experience.

"Chef," I began, interrupting his reverie.

"Yeah."

"I've been reading your e-mail."

It sneaked up on me, this spontaneous confession, and I immediately panicked. Here's where he puts out his cigarette in silence, I thought, and walks to the bedroom to pack. Or maybe he kicks over a table or dumps me out of the hammock onto the concrete. I had never seen him angry, although he had alluded to his temper. This was why he kept rubber bands around his wrist. Snap before you snap, was the theory. But I encountered none of this imagined rage. Instead, he looked right at me and smiled.

"I know."

I put one toe down on the cold concrete and set the hammock off rocking again.

"You've been reading it for months."

I swung in midair and waited for him to go on.

"At first I was ticked off," he explained, reaching for another cigarette. "And then I thought about it. Every one of my girlfriends has turned into a jealous psycho-bitch. It has to be something I'm doing."

We sat in silence for a while.

"So who is she?"

"Who is who?"

"You know who I'm talking about."

It was her mother's van we had driven to Vermont. It was she who sat in the salon in those tall black boots. She, I had to assume, owned a pair of leather pants.

"Was there anyone else?" I figured that I might as well get it out of the way now.

"A few, but nothing serious."

Well, at least I no longer had to feel quite as guilty about Leigh. Strength in numbers and all that jazz. But the knowledge that he had been seeing half of Manhattan made me wonder, with not a little anxiety, just how big a blind spot I was working with.

"And then the dust settled, chef," he went on, "and you were left standing."

Before reloading, I took a moment to savor the image of myself looking improbably good in chaps, with a revolver spinning around each forefinger.

"So why didn't it work?"

"We wanted different things."

"Yawn."

"Okay, she told me on our first date that she wanted to get married and have babies."

"To you?"

"No, not to me. Christ!" He sensed my rising panic and veered the subject to more general terms. "That's the thing about you New York women. You pretty much say what you want right up front."

"Really? Did I do that?"

"I could tell."

———

SOMEWHERE IN THAT conversation, life became very quiet. I had stopped narrating. When I looked at André, I saw the man sitting across from me, not his e-mails, his disappearances, the friends he kept to himself, or the calls he took in another room. This was my evidence: André in San Juan, smoking a cigarette, sitting across from no one else but me. And the little voice inside my head that was whispering to be patient.

"Are you ready for this?" he asked.

"Absolutely," I answered without hesitation.

"I'm a hard person to love."

I sat under the weight of his comment for a moment, wondering what he meant.

"I can do hard," I answered. "But I can't do unfaithful."

"Deal."

• A TIP •

If you want to change the majority of the components in a dish, you might consider choosing something else.

• city love •

AFTER WE LANDED in New York, André and I went back to our own apartments to drop off our things, but planned to rendezvous later. I arrived at the restaurant before he did, as usual. After a few minutes, I spotted him just outside the door, on his cell phone.

"That was my mother," he explained when he came in, scooting onto a stool. "I told her I was meeting you and she said 'Wasn't one week enough?'"

André's mother sounded like someone I would prefer to have on my side, if possible. If she and Leigh were close, as I suspected, this was not likely to be the case. After overhearing a conversation between André and his mother, I began to wonder if he had told her anything at all. Our little beach house in Puerto Rico had been gloriously quiet, so quiet that when she called one morning, I could hear the whole conversation from across the room.

"What are you doing down there?" she had asked. He an-

swered that we had been spending a lot of time at a little coffee shop across the street eating octopus salad, that we had
dinner last night at a place right on the beach, and that we
were planning on walking to Old San Juan later.

"Honey, that's a whole lot of 'we's,'" I heard her say. "And I
know you don't speak French."

As we sat at the bar and toasted our return to the city, I considered the extent to which our life might change now that it
was just the two of us. Would he introduce me to his mother?
Would I meet some of his wine friends? After seeing each other
for seven months, I felt as if we were just beginning.

Maybe because I was excited by this new beginning, I
dreaded going back to long shifts at the restaurant. I had become spoiled by our unscheduled week by the beach, going to
bed early and sleeping late, uninterrupted by meetings, e-mails,
and calls about reservations and purchase orders. Luckily, we
had a few days to readjust while the restaurant revved up for
the new year. The silverware needed unwrapping, the glasses
had to be polished and put back in their pristine rows, the
steam-cleaned chairs carried back into the dining room, and
the carpets and couches in the salon realigned on the newly
polished bronze floor.

At the end of one of these days, André invited me to his
apartment for the first time. About a block from his house, it
struck me that I really had no idea what his life looked like.
I had never seen his shower curtain or snooped in his refrigerator. Was he the type to fold his sweaters and arrange them
by color or did he pile them in his closet, along with the rest
of his wardrobe? As we walked down his tree-lined block, past
brownstones and six-figure cars, I began to pay close attention.
He stopped in front of a tall brick apartment building, steps
away from Central Park. Nice address, I thought to myself.

"You have an awning?" No one I knew had an awning, or at least no one I spent much time with.

"And a doorman in the evenings."

I loved my little place in Williamsburg, but my grimy, industrial street was a far cry from Central Park West. All I saw out of my window were warehouses and the thick forearms of the old woman across the street who sat in her window all day, occasionally leaning out to spit. André, on the other hand, lived in the land of the pedigreed dog and the space-age stroller. He could probably see the Sheep's Meadow in Central Park from his window, or even the Hudson River. I watched as he strolled casually through his mirrored lobby and pressed the button for the elevator. It didn't light up. This is what André's life looks like, I thought to myself. Someone will fix that button without his having to call or withhold his rent. These are André's neighbors, I thought as I studied the faces on the elevator. They probably work for firms of some sort and spend their days trading and merging and consolidating things. My neighbors used "freelance" as a verb. When we reached the fourth floor, I followed André down the hall and observed him putting his key into the lock on the door of apartment #402. He opened it and motioned for me to enter.

The apartment was literally the "coziest" apartment I had seen in my eight years in New York. It was the size of my dorm room in college—and that had bunk beds out of necessity. There was barely enough room to walk between the thick wooden frame of his beige futon and the piles of wine books stacked against the opposite wall. The floors were bare, the white walls were bare. In fact, the only thing close to decoration was a tie rack on which hung a rainbow of ties. His kitchen, which was about three steps from the edge of the futon, had little more than a pot, a frying pan, and an unopened can of breadcrumbs. But the four-star sommelier did have chilled Cava in the mini fridge and two Riedel champagne flutes.

"Here's to a new year," André said, holding up his glass.

"And to surviving the last," I answered as we clinked glasses.

I sat cross-legged on the futon, so as to conserve space, marveling at how much time I had wasted worrying about what my own life looked like. When André came to my place, I always wondered if he noticed my unvacuumed carpet, my overflowing bookshelves, and my refrigerator, which was filled with nothing but condiments. But at least I had owned a vacuum, a few bookshelves, and a full-size refrigerator. André fed an unmarked video into a TV/VCR the size of a toaster. It appeared to be a European soccer match and, from the short shorts, I put it somewhere around 1983. While he watched, I explored the rest of the apartment, namely the bathroom. There was a pea green toilet, a pea green tub, pea green tiles, and a clear shower curtain with sage green mold.

"You hate this, don't you?" André called, meaning the game.

"No, I really love the Cava."

"Come on," he said, shutting off the television. "Let's go to the diner."

His apartment did have the ideal location: the park in one direction and a twenty-four-hour diner in the other. Unfortunately, I had my doubts about the diner. In my opinion, a good diner must pass three tests. First, it must have more booths than tables. Second, the patty melt should be revered; I should not have to specify rye or choose a cheese. Most important, a chocolate milkshake must be made with chocolate ice cream—not vanilla with chocolate syrup—and it has to be served with the remaining shake in the silver blender cup in which it was made. I learned as a child that diners that skimp on that extra serving of milkshake should not be trusted. When I was young, diners were a place of worship, perhaps because the hamburger (later replaced by the superior patty melt), fries, and chocolate milkshake my parents allowed were like manna to a child who grew up on rabbits raised out back, potatoes from the garden, and homemade carob-chip cookies.

This judge gave André's diner a three. I penalized it for its slim selection of booths, its patty melt (shamefully flanked by white toast), and its meager and anemic chocolate shake in which I could not even stand a straw upright. Still, like André's micro-studio and our rocky start, I was determined to make it work.

EVENTUALLY, SERVICE AT Per Se began again in earnest. André and I went back into hiding, resuming our routine of restaurant-related dialogue with whispered subtext. Often, at the end of the night, André sidled up and asked, "Red, white, or bubbles?"

My wine selection would determine our late-night snack. Red could mean a home hot dog taste test. An off-dry white might inspire a little cheese. André liked to pair sparkling wine, or "bubbles," with the ten-ingredient fried rice we had delivered.

My life, which had revolved around my job for the last year, began to take place before and after Per Se. This might have been due, in part, to a new ease in the restaurant. With the review season well behind us, the dining room staff settled into a rhythm. My relations with the women backservers and runners were beginning to thaw, and I felt like I finally understood how to communicate with the chefs. Theoretically, I could now relax and perform the job I had worked so hard to learn.

One day, when it was my turn to come in early and iron, I decided to bring my iPod to help pass the time. I suspected this was against the rules, as I had never seen anyone but André wear headphones in the restaurant. His little bald head bobbing in front of his computer screen was a fixture in the office. Opting not to consult the two-page ironing procedure sheet to confirm the rules, on went the earphones and Johnny Cash pulled up a chair. In the starched and still dining room, his gravely drawl felt out of place. And suddenly, so did I. My shirt felt stiff, my tie too tight. The candy cane striped socks hidden under my black pants and the one silver bracelet inside my cuff were no longer enough. I wanted fire engine red hair and both arms loaded with the swath of silver bracelets André called my "body music." I wanted to swear and talk politics freely, eat Gray's Papaya hot dogs on the street and diner fries in a booth and disappear for days without telling anyone. When I began ironing the tables in the window, I looked enviously at the people reading the paper by the fountain. Shoppers hailed cabs. Across the circle, the ice cream truck held court—mercifully muted by the thick glass between us.

Any minute the other captains and backservers would begin to trickle in, carrying stacks of white plates and trays of silverware. I would slide my headphones into my jacket pocket and go in search of the flowers that we kept in the cool wine cellar overnight. After family meal, we would convene around the fireplace for the meeting, as we did before each service. The expediting chef would go through the three menus, describing lesser-known ingredients and techniques. After this, we'd be expected to ask questions. Inevitably someone would bring up something obscure just for the sake of asking. There was one captain who seemed to revel in subtle manipulation by pitting the chefs against each other. On days when he worked a double, he often asked a question at lunch, for example the base of a certain sauce, and then asked the same question at dinner. If two chefs answered differently, he would raise his hand again.

"I was just asking," he would say with concern, "because we were told at lunch that it was made with a veal reduction."

I could never quite understand what he got out of this, except perhaps a slight feeling of misplaced authority and the chance to see a chef squirm.

There was another character who gave great performances in meetings. This gentleman, Craig, was the sweetest, most devoted of servers, willing to do anything for his tables. He made them tea if they had a cold, rifled through the chocolate room to find the peanut butter truffle they craved, or ran to the maître d' stand for spare eyeglasses or a pashmina. Guests loved him. Chefs, on the other hand, found him infuriating because his questions always came from left field and often at exactly the wrong time. The rest of us loved comments like his apartment looking "like a homeless person lived there" or the table that kept him running all night by "drinking water like it was vodka." One day we were serving tripe as a first meat option. Most of the staff knew that was stomach, but up went a hand in the front row.

"Now, Chef," Craig asked, "exactly what kind of fish is a tripe?"

J.B. blew up and then launched into an epic lecture about product and professionalism. Poor Craig never lived it down.

The chefs had their own ticks and personalities in the meetings. Corey sped through the menu so fast that on weekend mornings, the sleepy staff could barely keep up. J.B. demarcated the size of smaller ingredients by placing the tip of his thumb on the fleshy part of his ring finger or pinky. A marble potato, for example, put his thumb just above the joint. When a dish had "a little heat to it," he fanned his mouth as if simulating a Cherokee war cry. When Corey moved to Napa to become the chef de cuisine at the French Laundry, he was replaced at the pass by a chef we all adored, Chris L'Hommedieu. Chris's approach was more relaxed than any of the other chefs. When the managers put pressure on him to quiz us on the menu, he chose questions that, in a game of *Jeopardy!*, would be an easy $200.

The wine team followed the chef with a list of items we were out of. Sometimes they suggested wines for each course, sometimes they called on captains to make suggestions for a pairing. Certain captains were better at this than others. I, as you might imagine, was not one of the better ones.

If André ran the meeting, he went easy on me, asking me to pair something with the dishes we had seen thousands of times, like the Oysters and Pearls or the foie gras torchon. Sometimes he asked me about a wine we had just tasted the night before. Often he slipped in little inside jokes, commenting on how hard it had been to get out of bed that morning, taking a poll on whether people turned the heat down at night (I did, he didn't), asking if anyone had seen the movie we had just watched. Just when the managers started to look peeved, he would segue effortlessly into a wine-related topic. When it was our turn to ask questions, I tried to get him back.

At one time these meetings had terrified me, and I had feigned interest in my heinous shoes in the hopes of not being called on. Now I was quiet for a different reason. I had welcomed spring lamb at the start of two springs. After two summers, the sweet corn pudding had become an old friend. Twice, tomatoes came and went, as did ramps and fiddleheads and wild asparagus. Not only did I know the biographies, philosophies, and eccentricities of our main purveyors, I had met or waited on many of them.

Beginning on that afternoon of ironing, I began toying with the idea of leaving Per Se. I loved working as a waiter, but I certainly didn't want to be doing it when I was fifty, or if I ever chose to have a family, unless I could put my baby in a papoose or feed my kids at one of the tables. There were a few big restaurant openings rumored in the city and I considered hopping around, working the first six months in a series of restaurants until I came up with a better idea. Poor Mr. Bruni would be very confused. On further consideration, I concluded that nothing would compare to opening Per Se. Another option to spice things up would be to work toward a promotion, but I didn't see myself as the management type. As for being a maître d', I had little patience for the who's-who aspect of the job. I had no real interest in—or talent for—the historical or business sides of wine, so being a sommelier was also out. The only other career I could think of in restaurants would be reviewing, but knowing as many people as I did in New York restaurants by now, I would have to move. For the first time since I had started working at Per Se, I began to drag my feet when coming to work and wish my guests would hurry up and eat so I could go home.

Until now, school had always come second to the restaurant. I read on the subway, I wrote stories the morning I handed them in. Soon after starting at Per Se, I began to write about the restaurant, mostly because I worked seventy-hour weeks and thought about nothing but food, stars, and my coworkers. I had no big plans for these stories, but the more I wrote, the more came to me. Sometimes when feeling particularly itchy, I tried to think of work as research for class.

Another shift in consciousness took place between André

and me. No longer did we talk about Per Se alone. He met more of my friends outside of the business; I met a few of his wine contacts. We spent late nights contemplating our respective, and shared, futures after Per Se. And we began to plan our next vacation. The closure was still five months away, but it became one of our favorite topics of conversation. We thought about wine regions, hitting a few Michelin three-star restaurants, fulfilling my fantasy of living on a houseboat in France, but then André had a suggestion that sounded perfect. A road trip.

"It should have a theme. Like food-on-a-stick."

André looked repulsed.

"Diners? Pie? How about roadside attractions?"

In my collage of America there are drive-ins, fairs, rodeos, bowling alleys, towns with crazy names, and ice cream socials, but I think most of those faded with the advent of color television. André's America was a very different place, I noted when he offered a suggestion.

"How about motels with vibrating beds?"

In the next five months, we didn't officially live together, but we began to divide our time between our "pied à terre" in the city and our "country house" in Brooklyn. This meant that André's apartment needed a little attention. I assumed that Leigh took most of the amenities with her because until I brought over my duvet, there was nothing on the futon but a pilled fleece blanket that either covered our shoulders or our feet—not both. I bought a standing lamp, so as to avoid the fluorescent ceiling lighting, and a stovetop espresso maker, so as to survive. Other than that, I tried to let André run his household as he pleased. One morning, he was rushing to get ready for work while I lounged, having commandeered his half of the mini-blanket. He tended to go in midmorning, while I didn't have to be there until three o'clock. Sometimes I stayed at his place, wrote for a while, and slipped him his keys later at work.

"Do you want me to do anything?" I called to him.

"Do you want to iron some shirts?"

"Not really."

He had meant the request to be a joke. We both knew I would not be ironing his shirts. I assumed that this was one more way Leigh and I differed. She nicknamed herself "Henrietta Housewife"; I didn't even own an ironing board. She liked to cook; I liked to eat out. She did the laundry; I dropped mine off. If he wanted a domestic goddess, he would be disappointed. And if he expected me to stay home while he went to restaurant openings and wine dinners, I would be more than disappointed, I would be out of there. My idea of hell was waking up in the middle of suburbia with frosted hair and cakey makeup, making English muffin pizzas for my children as they zoned in front of the television or fought over video games and then grew up to be pharmaceutical lobbyists or vegans.

At one time, I would have preferred for André to go to work and leave me with my solitary morning. Now, I wanted to pull on a pair of jeans, tame my Little Prince hair, and head over to the diner. Given the size of André's place, the diner became an annex of sorts. Sometimes, on days when he didn't have to be at the restaurant until late, we got up early, had breakfast, and then went back to bed. In the mornings, children in booster seats ate French toast with sticky fingers, well-worn couples silently divided the paper, and old men in argyle ate corned beef hash, as they should. My favorite part of the breakfast menu was the muffin selection: blueberry muffin, corn muffin, banana-nut muffin, bran mjuffin. I liked this section for two reasons. The first was that spelling errors—not my own—always make me feel a little superior. Also, I like muffins because they are really just an excuse to eat cake in the morning.

"You want coffee?" the harried waiter always barked, hurling napkins, silverware, water glasses, and menus onto the table as if we had asked for too much already. André and I made up Seven Dwarf names for all the waiters here; this one we called Grumpy because when he was not berating a coworker, he had his head stuck in the window to the kitchen. His words were lost amid the scraping of spatulas on the grill and the roar of the dishwasher, but his flailing arms were a good indication of the tone. Sleepy ran the cash register, resting her drooping head on the palm of her hand so that her coarse, overdyed hair fell dangerously close to the bowl of mints on the counter. The mints seemed always to have been picked over, leaving only neon lemon and licorice.

"Coffee would be great," I answered, shrinking into the booth. I read carefully, trying to remember what I meant to have the last time. I only ordered from the Griddle Specialties column when I remembered to bring my own maple syrup. This might never have occurred to me had it not been for a nondescript blue-haired old woman who we watched fish a bunch of plastic supermarket spice containers from her handbag one morning. Once she had them in place on the table, she carefully pried open each spice (or unscrewed, depending on the tops), smelled them, and gently dusted her meal.

André and I had a recurrent conversation, no matter the hour.

André: I am going to ask what the hamburger patty is.

Phoebe: It's a hamburger with no bun, served with eggs any style, home fries, and toast.

But he would still ask, as if running his own little experiment. I think he liked the thought of getting himself a reputation, even if said reputation was being illiterate and a little dim. In the end, he always ordered the usual: egg, cheese, sausage, and bacon on a roll. If I forgot my syrup, I might have poached eggs on an English muffin, which I allowed to get nice and soggy before I began.

André's lease was up at the end of January and mine at the end of February, but we both agreed that it was too early to think about officially moving in together. He needed some time to get used to ironing his own shirts again, and we both needed the option of going home alone. This did not mean, in my opinion, that there weren't baby steps that could be taken between casual dating and moving in together. In the continuum of many New York relationships, the bestowal of keys falls between becoming exclusive and the popping of certain questions. Exclusivity must be established because while "in flagrante delicto" has a nice ring, that is just about all it has going for it.

Once this is settled, preparations for key exchange can begin. The bestower is wise to dispose of anything sordid and all evidence of relationships past. This includes erasing browser histories; clearing the digital camera; combing the apartment for renegade hairs; establishing passwords for the BlackBerry, Palm, or cell; lowering the volume on the answering machine; and alerting potential callers.

Key privileges come with their own set of responsibilities: refraining from organizing, rearranging, and doing laundry. Groceries, however, are welcomed. If the recipient has not introduced a toothbrush permanently, now is the time. It is not yet time for a drawer. I had a toothbrush and an overnight bag that spent the night at André's even when I didn't, but I did not have a drawer. Nor did I have keys. This meant that on days when I was not working, or nights when I got out before he did, I had to wait somewhere. For this reason alone, I began to frequent the diner without André.

BESIDES MY WORKPLACES, I had never spent as much time in a single restaurant as I did in that diner. I got to know it so well that I began to feel that it had replaced Per Se as the set for the reality television show that was my life. From four stars to no stars, from silver to stainless, from crystal to tinted glass, I felt as if I were stepping back into the real world.

Between two o'clock in the morning and daybreak, the city that never sleeps sometimes nods off. As I sat in the diner window looking out, the streets were quiet. A few cabs sped by now and then on Broadway and the occasional lumbering garbage truck wove down a cross street. I'd experienced diverse social circles during my time in New York, but the predawn diner crowd was a new one. At this hour, single men read twenty-five-cent papers, the occasional cop had a coffee at the counter, and postconcert Juilliard students discussed vocal exercises over grilled cheese. I always placed my cell phone on the top left quadrant of the table so that I would hear it when it chirped, alerting me that André was on his way. Below my phone, a vase of plastic flowers, loosely modeled after daisies, snuggled close to a newish bottle of ketchup. I was briefly reminded of the floral arrangements at work, expressly chosen to be seen and not smelled. My water glass reminded me of tinted eyeglasses that darken in the sunlight.

The menu was about the same dimensions as Per Se's, albeit brown vinyl with plastic pages. Unlike some diner menus, this one did not feature the segmented page where specials are stuck into slots like shoes in one of those shoe organizer things that hang from your closet door. They wrote their specials on a dry-erase board in multicolored letters: matzoh ball soup, gray sole filet, beef goulash. I never ordered the specials. I did once order almost every dessert—minus the cream pies—just to know what I was up against. The apple pie had clearly been baked in anticipation of a slow death in the glass cabinet behind the counter and had been heavily embalmed with cinnamon and allspice. Desert-dry layers of the chocolate cake were held gallantly together by an icing so pasty and thick that elementary schools might consider it an alternative to that gloppy adhesive the kids eat anyway.

I imagined that many regulars never even consulted a menu. The only real reason to even read a diner menu is to remind yourself of what you already know is there and hope to be surprised. Here, hidden between the Greek salad, the hot openface turkey sandwich, and the Diet Delights (most of which included cottage cheese or Jell-O) was a bison burger. It was followed by a tiny nutritional table in which the fat, calories, and cholesterol were measured against its chicken, turkey, and beef counterparts. I imagined many a paunchy truck driver felt quite proud of his choice, after opting for the leaner, protein-packed bison. Blintzes also seemed out of place, as did the jelly omelet, but my recent discovery that the blueberry pancakes actually contained blueberries, as opposed to cowering under gelatinous blueberry goo, was a welcome surprise.

Another highlight of this menu were the illustrations that flirted from the margins—the kinds of things your mother was supposed to make: pork chops with mashed potatoes and gravy, roast chicken, a pie with curlicues rising from the crust, signifying the sweet smell of nostalgia. It occurred to me that I should master an upstanding and moral meal of this sort, should I prove key-worthy.

My preoccupation with André's keys was not about access to

his 150-square-foot studio apartment. It was not about the futon that served as couch, bed, desk, kitchen table, and ironing
board, or the overenthusiastic radiator, or the sneezing Japanese man who lived next door, or the microwave that smelled
like popcorn even when not in use. Such milestones as keys
or rings or pins or shared pets or important introductions are
more about momentum than they are about the object or occurrence. I believe that this is what women mean when they
talk about the relationship "going somewhere." Because if it is
not going somewhere, they will be going somewhere—taking
their roast chicken with them, lest they wind up with cankles
and *National Geographic* breasts, the single parent of cats.

THE MORE TIGHTLY André and I wove our lives outside of
Per Se, the more I wanted to meet 2040. It didn't matter how in
love with me he was, or how many other women he had dated
in New York, or the fact that she was now seeing someone else;
I needed to know that we had no more secrets. I brought this
up a few times and André answered that we were certain to
run into one another at some point. From his tone, it seemed
he wasn't looking forward to this.

And then one day, he informed me that we had been invited
over for dinner. I froze.

"Wasn't that what you wanted?" he asked.

I had, indeed, wanted to meet her, but spending an entire
evening at her apartment was more than I had bargained for.
Still, I figured I should be glad that he felt comfortable with
our meeting in such an intimate setting.

"She loves to cook!" he shouted from the shower on the
night of our dinner, making it sound as if we were doing her a
favor by allowing her to cook for us.

"It'll go fine—she's very likable." He assured me as we walked toward the subway. "She lives in a great neighborhood, but it takes forever to get there. I usually take a crosstown bus." The word *usually* induced a spell of heart-racing and nausea.

"This is a terrible idea," a friend said, after I told her what I knew about 2040, including her desire for children, culinary expertise, and choice in pants. "This woman sounds like a walking womb. Can't you just meet for a drink?"

I imagined 2040 standing in the doorway like a peasant in an impressionist wheat field, breasts spilling from a lazily laced bodice, blond curls begging for release, eyes adoring— yet capable, loin throbbing with the anticipation of lineage.

André's familiarity with the route, with the intercom, with the finicky elevator made him a stranger. Fortunately for him, it made him the alluring kind of stranger. The kind who causes a girl to miss her stop on the train.

2040 and the man she was seeing—whom we all nicknamed "Big A," with his reluctant consent—had nearly polished off a bottle of wine by the time we arrived. She was a husky-voiced, minimalist version of my impressionist nightmare. By minimalist, I mean she lacked the bodice and wheat field; the breasts, locks, and inviting loin remained. André and I settled into the couch, which separated the living area from the open kitchen. Glasses in hand, we all toasted and proceeded to act as if we knew very little about one another. I watched André and 2040, André watched 2040 and me, 2040 watched André and me, and Big A ran down to his car to get some CDs.

"I'm sorry. He's not the kind of guy I usually date," she said, leaning close.

Obviously, I thought. André was certainly not a Big A. The thought of her ever being single set my heart racing again.

"We really don't have that much in common. I mean, he sells cars."

She got up to stir something simmering on the stove. Big A came back with a pile of CDs.

"I hear you're a writer," said 2040, changing the subject. Even though she faced her cauldron, I knew this was directed toward me. I narrowed my eyes at André.

"What are you writing about?"

Not liking to discuss my writing with strangers, I had been privately auditioning possible conversation stoppers, but I didn't think that I would ever have the nerve to use one. But now, in the most awkward of situations, it seemed appropriate.

"Actually, I'm writing a biography," I responded casually. "About a man in Alaska who makes foie gras from penguins."

Now, if this were the movies, André would have sprayed his mouthful of wine across the coffee table. Instead, he looked mortified; 2040 looked disgusted and went on stirring.

I considered detailing the anti–foie gras legislation up for debate in California, bogus Alaskan food regulations, biographical information for my ex-funeral-pianist hero named Mr. Dirge, and the working title: *Bing and Dirge*. Instead, I buried my face in my glass and hoped to be rescued.

"She scares me," Big A announced.

André asked Big A the kind of questions one is supposed to ask a man who sells cars, questions about models and years and names that sounded to me like screen names for Internet porn. Lacking a driver's license, I chose wisely, if a little too late, to remain silent. On the other hand, 2040 piped in from the stove about some difficulties she had been having with her scooter. I imagined André behind her on the leather seat and grew nauseated again.

As 2040 served mussels, then escargots, then mushroom soup, I felt like the kind of New York woman who wears black in July and does most of her shopping at the corner deli, both of which were true. Before the filet mignon and cheese courses,

I offered to wash some dishes. André raised an eyebrow, and I tried to remember if he had ever seen me scrub a pot.

"You don't have to do that," she said, waving dismissively toward the stack of red clay tapas dishes in the sink.

I washed, Big A dried. He stopped trying to be funny, I stopped pretending to have it together.

"You working on any other books?" he teased.

"In fact I am," I responded. "I'm writing a children's book."

"Pickled baby seals and actual Eskimo pies?"

"No, it's called *Where's Daddy?*"

The group let that one be.

"Did she hate me?" I whined on the bus ride home.

"How could she hate you?" André reassured me. "She said you were cooler than she thought you would be."

"I'm not sure if that's a compliment to either of us."

We stared silently out the window for a while, watching our previous route rewind. Then André took my hand and kissed the center of my palm in the way that I love.

"Chef? I think your book concepts need a little work."

"JUST YOU TONIGHT?"

"For now," I responded, trying to sound like I didn't mind either way. My waiter looked at me carefully and nodded. As my favorite of the diner dwarfs, he had been spared a derogatory name. He moved quickly, despite the limp in his right leg, which caused it to drag behind him as if he had a small child attached to it that he was determined to ignore. Late at night he worked alone and performed the same routine at every new table.

"Hello!" he said casually to his victim as he sidled up. "Coffee?" At that moment, in swooped the (empty) cup and saucer, which he had been holding just out of the guests' line of sight until this moment. He fumbled and faked panic, pretending to overturn the cup (firmly secured by his ring finger through the handle).

"Oops!" he cried as they all shrieked and threw up their hands. Tonight a bunch of rowdy tourists threatened to sue. One woman fanned herself with her menu for a good five minutes afterward. He winked at me.

I ordered some coffee and was spared the comedy act. Some of it sloshed into the saucer en route, meaning that I either risked staining by drip (or neck injury from trying to dodge the drip) or I would have to use my one allocated napkin to soak it up. I ordered some toast. It arrived looking perfectly plastic, accompanied by ice cold butter in those silly little plastic tubs with the bendable tab that slices under your thumb-nail. I looked mournfully down at the grape jelly and realized that I was going to have to start bringing my own jam. Come to think of it, I might as well bring a whole van of everything I might need to exist in the land of no stars: maple syrup, jam, extra napkins, a decent staff. Hell, why not go ahead and bring a pepper grinder? I was beginning to get nice and bothered when I heard a tapping on the window. André grinned and waved.

"You need a menu?" a voice called from across the room once he had settled into the chair across from me.

"No. No, I don't." He ordered his usual egg, cheese, sausage, and bacon on a roll and the waiter limped over to the kitchen window to call in the order. André leaned in close, his face triumphant.

"Did you hear that?"

"Hmmm," I responded, trying to decide whether the western omelet deserved a chance. "Aren't you going to ask what the hamburger patty is?"

"No. I don't think I need to anymore. After all, we're regulars now."

Now that was a milestone I didn't see coming.

• A TIP •

Tip 20 percent or more. Two extra dollars mean very little to you, but they are a compliment to your server.

• service included •

O N   O U R   S U M M E R road trip there were no vibrating beds, ice cream socials, or rodeos, and the closest thing we had to food-on-a-stick was a turkey leg in Memphis—and still, we had a blast. But when we returned to work after the vacation, Chef Keller had a surprise for us. Beginning in September, the restaurant would institute a 20 percent service charge on every check and pay the staff a negotiated hourly salary. No sooner had he uttered the news than it had been heralded from gossip pages, foodie Web sites, CNN, the *New Yorker*, and newspapers from L.A. to New York.

Very few of us had worked in such a system, although it is common in Europe, and used in a handful of American restaurants such as Chez Panisse in Berkeley, Charlie Trotter in Chicago, and, before it closed, the Quilted Giraffe in New York. Chef Keller sold the new policy to the staff as a means of equalizing a fairly dramatic income discrepancy between the cooks and the waiters. There's hardly a restaurant in the city for which this discrepancy isn't the case and, in most restaurants, it creates an undercurrent of resentment between the front and back of the house. A line cook working sixty hours a week might have gone to culinary school and have tens of thousands of dollars in student loans while some actor with no pertinent schooling works half the hours and makes twice as much.

It was easy to feel compassion for the cooks, but when those of us at the top end of the pay scale realized we stood to lose about a quarter of our income, the tone changed. Some of the captains and backservers bemoaned the pricey vacations they had just taken. Others worried about tuition for their children for which they had already budgeted. In an effort at damage control, the management informed the staff that if a guest left extra gratuity, half of that sum would go to the captain and half would be split among the rest of the dining room staff. This sounded dangerously like a handshake to me, which had never worked in my favor.

There was much grumbling. If the managers had a problem with how much the cooks were being paid, some of the dining room staff said under their breath, then they should pay them more. One of the captains questioned where the money was *really* going. We had been told that some of it would be reserved for raises and year-end gifts.

"Keep the Christmas cookbook," he suggested sarcastically. "I'll take the cash."

Having management involved in the distribution of gratuity itself would take getting used to. In almost every other restaurant in the city, the staff divided earnings themselves. Now, we would be turning that responsibility over without full understanding of how it would be distributed. But, because of the way the news had been spun, to voice our objection made us seem greedy and unwilling to share with the debt-ridden, malnourished, practically homeless chefs in the kitchen.

Once the sticker shock wore off, we began to think about how this might affect the service standards in the restaurant. If it took the same effort to open a thirty-dollar bottle of wine as it did to open a three-thousand-dollar bottle, didn't they worry about sales incentives? What if they cut back the staff to save money? Would we now have larger stations and more covers with no more compensation? How would our relationship with the guests change? Would they be resentful of being told how much to tip? How would they feel about 20 percent being added to the price of their wine? Would it change our relationship as a staff? Would people start to fight over the extra tippers?

I was torn. I supported increasing the chefs' incomes, and the idea of being compensated like any other industry was certainly appealing. Being paid like a professional eased that sneaking feeling of servitude. I would still make enough to live comfortably in New York. Even after the pay cut, my salary was three times that at which most people started in publishing. But I began to ask myself: if it weren't for the money, would I stay? A year ago, the answer would have been, without hesitation, yes.

One day in August, after I had been pondering this question for a few weeks, I walked through the kitchen and spotted one of Chef Keller's many signs. It was affixed to the wall by a tidy border of green tape (tape at Per Se was cut, not torn). The sign read: WHAT WOULD YOU DO IF YOU KNEW YOU COULD NOT FAIL? When I had looked up at that sign in the past, I always thought of Per Se as a whole. We had achieved four stars already and in the coming year, we would achieve five Mobil stars and three Michelin stars as well. We didn't fail because we met our own standards and, thankfully, our standards aligned with those of our critics. Someone asked me recently what I thought set Per Se apart. Accountability, I answered. My coworkers never let sloppiness or carelessness slide. God help the runner who dropped food to the wrong positions, the bartender who took too long making his homemade tonic water, the backserver who let a table go without water, a captain whose table asked for their check. Chances are, his coworkers would say something before management had a chance to be diplomatic.

This time, when I looked up at the sign, the question felt much more personal.

On my break between shifts, I sat by the fountain in front of the Time Warner Center and made a list of reasons to stay and reasons to quit. Stay: income, writing material, time with André. Quit: time, freedom, new haircut.

"Is this irresponsible?" I asked André after work when I had all but made my decision. "Am I being too impulsive? It's entirely possible that I'll never make this kind of money again. What if I use up all my savings and have to live on canned dog food and sleep in a box in the park?"

"I'm sure you could get a job at TGI Friday's before it got that bad."

"What if we don't have anything to talk about anymore?"

"Well, we should probably find that out sooner rather than later."

After I put in my notice, a friend who had just broken off her engagement asked if she could stay at my apartment in Brooklyn while she looked for her own place. Her crushing devastation could not have come at a better time. She moved into my place and I officially moved into André's.

I was glad to pack only a few things at first. There was hardly room in his apartment for the two of us, let alone my books and furniture. The gradual move-in would allow me to slowly wean myself from my little haven in Brooklyn, where I had once closed the door and been perfectly alone. After I packed one small bag, I settled into my couch corner for a moment. Across the room stood the old wooden desk that I had convinced my ex to carry on the subway from a Chelsea thrift shop. This reminded me of how I had begged him, not long after that, to haul a worn, white bureau from the stoop sale down the street, up the four flights of stairs. It wanted a coat of paint, but instead I replaced its drawer handles with bright, mismatched porcelain knobs, a look reminiscent of an eccentric old woman in costume jewelry. Next to the desk was an old velvet chair of robin's-egg blue that I kept safe for a friend now living in New Orleans. By my feet sat the wooden chest I had claimed from my parents' house. For some reason, I thought of the morning I woke up to bird's wings, a sound e. e. cummings had likened to clouds whispering. I had left the window open the night before when I crawled in from the fire escape. More memories haunted my solitude and by the time I closed the door to my apartment, I was sobbing.

The few pairs of jeans I had packed barely fit into André's little corner cupboard, and I had to displace a few nonessentials to fit my minimal cosmetics into the pea green bathroom. I crammed a sweater into the suitcase where he kept his, the one that sat on the stacked milk crates housing his wine collection. I squeezed a few skirts and nice pants to the right of his suits and dress shirts, and hung two belts, a brown and a black, from a nail in his closet. My Le Creuset Dutch oven took up residence on the stovetop. Now that I had proven key-worthy, it was time to master the meals drawn in the margins of the diner menu, the ones your mother was supposed to make.

My landlord agreed to let me out of my lease in January, a month ahead of schedule, which meant that we had four months of sardine living ahead of us while we planned our next move. Strangely enough, now that I had arrived, I couldn't have been happier at the prospect.

"I think it might be time for a dachshund," I casually mentioned one night.

"French bulldog."

"Whatever."

• a few more tips •

Don't try to bribe the host. If there's no table, there's no table.

•

"Do you know who I am?" is a very unattractive question.

•

Consider storing your handbag under your chair where we won't step on it.

•

Take a moment to listen to your waiter when she offers to tell you about the menu or take your water, cocktail, or food order. If you are in the middle of an important conversation, let her know and make eye contact when you are ready. No need to be rude.

•

You may have ordered your signature cocktail a million times, but we need time to write when you say "dirtybombaysapphiremartiniupextradryandvery-chillednoolives."

•

See if everyone at the table is ready to order before you begin and that everyone is finished eating before you request to be cleared.

•

We are happy to split your check, but it helps when you tell us up front. You'd be surprised at how complicated it can be to make changes on some computers.

•

"Give me . . ." is a very unattractive way to begin a sentence.

•

When you don't like something, don't get mad at your waiter. He didn't make it.
Having said that, please give us your opinions about the restaurant, both negative and positive, so that we can tell the chef or the management.

•

Do not touch your waiter.

•

Adding people to your party is not in the Diner's
Bill of Rights.

•

Try to consolidate your requests.

•

When a waiter seems to be ignoring you, most likely
it is because a fellow guest got to her first, not that
she is incompetent, unkind, or unintelligent.

•

Do not pick up your glass when a waiter or sommelier
is about to pour something for you. It makes you
seem greedy and oblivious.

•

Your food is delivered to your table based on where
you were sitting when we took the order. When you
switch seats, it screws us all up.

•

Please don't ask us for cigarettes.

•

Larger glasses appear less full than smaller glasses. This does not mean you are getting less wine.

Never get up and take something from a waiter's station. That includes water pitchers, coffee pitchers, silverware, napkins, and pens. Please do not steal our pens. Usually we have to provide our own.

Do not put your napkin on your dirty plate.

Control your limbs.

Please don't involve us in your monetary disputes. Do not shove cash in our pockets or aprons, or wrench credit cards from our hands.

Don't hold your waiter responsible if someone else beat you to paying for dinner.

When he found newspaper, wrapping paper, or Kleenex on the table, a waiter friend in Brooklyn used to grumble, "Yo mama don't live here."

• afterword: my dinner with andré •

ANDRÉ AND I had dinner at Per Se a few months af-ter I left. In the days leading up to our reservation, I thought often of possible menus, possible nonsuit wardrobe choices, and possible awkward moments. Everyone at the res-taurant knew about André and me by now, but it would be the first time we made an official appearance together.

We took our usual route from the apartment, down Central Park West. As we walked, we wondered aloud about what we knew would be an epic meal. Would we sit in the window or upstairs on a banquette? Would there be truffles? Hot or cold foie gras? About two blocks from the Trump Tower, André el-bowed me.

"Is that who I think it is?"

It was the zaniest and most trying of regulars, a petit and very bald gentleman who went by only one name and always spoke about himself in the third person. For example, when accosted with the bill: —— never pays for truffles. Or, when denied a table for the next night: There's always a table for ——! Upon spotting us, he said a quick hello and then accused us of avoiding him on the street in Williamsburg, an instance I had almost forgotten about and assumed we had gotten away with. And then, in typical —— fashion, he forgave us and offered us the wine he had left at Per Se a few months before. Apparently, —— no longer paid for wine, either. It was a shock to be included in the Per Se posse of regulars, if only by association. We declined his offer and beat a hasty retreat.

When we arrived at the restaurant, a host led us to one of the two banquettes that overlook the dining room, the park, and the lights from East Side high-rises. None of the formalities would be skipped during our meal, even though we could easily have found our way to table twenty-three and poured ourselves the champagne we knew would be chilling in the bucket. I couldn't help marveling at it all—at the room, at my colleagues who glided through the room, at my intimacy with each detail of the service, at the fact that, despite this intimacy, I had completely forgotten to check whether the logo on the base of my champagne flute had been set at six o'clock.

We sipped the champagne and ate our salmon cornets, in the recommended two to three bites. "Did you ever imagine . . . ?" I started to ask André, before a stream of managers, maître d's, captains, backservers, runners, and coffee servers stopped by to welcome us, to pour more champagne, and to inform us that the chef wanted to cook for us.

Did we have any allergies? No.

Any dislikes? None worth holding on to.

Time constraints? Absolutely not.

Some diners find the concept of an unknown menu to be frightening. I know this because I have seen the stricken look on their faces. But to me, a restaurant with no menu, headed by a chef I trusted, would be ideal. In such a utopia, guests could specify deathly allergies, hunger level, and time constraints, but then they would unfurl their napkin and surrender. Imagine a room full of real eaters, willing to try something they usually hate, at the mercy of a chef whose only limit is her imagination (and possibly red tide). It would be like the director or actor whose films you see, the author whose books you buy in hardcover as soon as they hit the shelves, or the musicians whose concert tickets you are willing to sleep on the sidewalk to buy. You might skim the reviews and take friends' opinions into consideration, but you trust the director, author, artist, or chef far more.

It was a wonderful meal, all seventeen courses and six hours of it, in part because its creators knew our palates all too well. Sweetbreads, seared foie gras, and carrot cake go in André's favorite foods of all time. The presence of bone marrow on my plate did not go unnoticed. Neither did the truffles, in separate but equal portions so as not to inspire jealousy. The two caviar presentations were new to us, and both equally astounding. When we were ready to begin to move toward sweets, pastry sent the thyme ice cream, a dish that I had served so many times but never tried. It arrives with a thin disk of chocolate covering the bowl. Then, whoever is serving it puts a few grains of salt in the center of the chocolate and then drizzles hot Provençal olive oil, which melts a hole in the disk and drops the salt onto the ice cream. It was as arresting a combination of flavors as I had imagined.

I have no doubt that I will eat all over the world in my lifetime, but I have my loyalties. The evening André and I spent at Per Se, coddled by the kitchen and our colleagues, will be the memory to which I will compare the rest.

---

per se menu

November 13, 2005

André's Menu

PURÉE OF BROCCOLI SOUP

Broccoli Florettes and Pickled Pearl Onions

RUSSIAN SEVRUGA CAVIAR

Red Marble Potatoes and Kendall Farm's Crème Fraîche

GEODUCK CLAM

Heirloom Radish Ribbons and Ponzu Glaze

GRILLED FRENCH SARDINE

Saffron-Braised Cauliflower, Shaved Fennel Bulb,
and Piquillo Peppers

TOAD IN THE HOLE

Brioche with Quail Egg and Black Winter Truffle Emulsion

MÉDAILLON DE RIS DE VEAU

Honey-Braised Cranberries, Glazed Sunchokes, Pissenlit,
and Veal Sauce

SALAD OF GRILLED RED ONIONS
Poached Pink Lady Apples and Black Winter Truffle Vinaigrette

MASCARPONE-ENRICHED CHESTNUT AGNOLOTTI
Shaved White Truffles from Alba

HERB-ROASTED TURBOT RÔTI SUR LE DOS
Celery Root Fondant, Shaved Celery Branch, and Confit of Ruby Red
Grapefruit with Burgundy Truffle Fondue

PEAS AND CARROTS
Nova Scotia Lobster Cuit Sous Vide
Sweet Carrot Parisienne, Pea Shoot Salad, and Carrot Butter

PAN-ROASTED SCOTTISH RED LEG PARTRIDGE
Sautéed Hudson Valley Moulard Duck Foie Gras
Matignon of Root Vegetables and Sauce Périgourdine

SNAKE RIVER FARM'S CALOTTE DE BOEUF GRILLÉE
Forty-Eight-Hour Braised Wagyu Beef Brisket,
Crispy Bone Marrow, Young Leeks, Black Trumpet Mushrooms, and
Salsify Root with Sauce Bordelaise

PETITE ARDI-GASNA
Flowering Quince Membrillo, Grilled Cipollini Onion Rings,
Sweet Pepper Vinaigrette, and Blue Moon Acres Mezza Arugula

SORBET À L'HUILE D'OLIVE
Chocolate Pudding and Niçoise Olive Oil

MANGO SORBET
Passion Fruit Caramel Ganache, Croustillant, and White
Chocolate Granité

SWEET GARDEN CARROT CAKE
Vanilla Cream Cheese Icing, Candied Walnut Crust, Black Raisin
Coulis, and Indonesian Cinnamon Ice Cream

CHOCOLATE SPICED CARAMEL
Valrhona Chocolate Brownie, Milk Chocolate Ganache, Milk
Chocolate Snow Flakes, Spiced Caramel Ice Cream, and Caramel Jam

MIGNARDISES

Phoebe's Menu

PURÈE OF PARSNIP SOUP
Bosc Pear Brunoise

RUSSIAN SEVRUGA CAVIAR
Compressed English Cucumber, Kaffir Lime Gelée,
and Lemon Cream

CITRUS-CURED HIRAMASA
Scallion Salad and Persimmon Aigre-Doux

ROASTED TURBOT CHEEK
Sweet Pepper Fondue and Crisp Pancetta

WHITE TRUFFLE OIL–INFUSED CUSTARD
with Ragoût of Périgord Truffles

WARM LAMB'S TONGUE
Lamb Ribette, Sweet Carrot Ribbons, and Medjool Date

SALAD OF SHAVED FENNEL BULB
Slow-Baked Heirloom Beets and Black Winter Truffle Vinaigrette

MASCARPONE-ENRICHED CHESTNUT AGNOLOTTI
Shaved White Truffles from Alba

HERB-ROASTED TURBOT RÔTI SUR LE DOS
Celery Root Fondant, Shaved Celery Branch, and Confit of Ruby Red
Grapefruit with Burgundy Truffle Fondue

SWEET BUTTER–POACHED SCOTTISH LANGOUSTINES
Miso-Glazed Eggplant, Grilled Lemongrass, and Oxtail Emulsion

PAN-ROASTED SCOTTISH RED LEG PARTRIDGE
Sautéed Hudson Valley Moulard Duck Foie Gras,
Matignon of Root Vegetables, and Sauce Périgourdine

SNAKE RIVER FARM'S CALOTTE DE BOEUF GRILLÉE
Forty-Eight-Hour Braised Wagyu Beef Brisket,
Crispy Bone Marrow, Young Leeks, Black Trumpet Mushrooms,
and Salsify Root with Sauce Bordelaise

BREBIS DES PYRÉNÉES
Belgian Endive Marmalade, Périgord Truffle Shortbread,
and Red Beet Essence

GARDEN THYME–INFUSED ICE CREAM
Chocolate Tuile, Fleur de Sel, and Moulin Des Pénitents
Extra Virgin Olive Oil

BANANA SORBET
Jamaican Rum Cake, Cassia Foam, and Kaffir Lime Leaf Custard

SWEET GARDEN CARROT CAKE
Vanilla Cream Cheese Icing, Candied Walnut Crust, Black Raisin
Coulis, and Indonesian Cinnamon Ice Cream

PER SE SACHER TORTE
Chocolate Pain de Gênes, Apricot Marmalade, Ginger Custard,
Apricot Ice Cream, and Juniper Berry Gelée with Spiced Bread
Nougatine

MIGNARDISES

• acknowledgments •

Most sincerely, I want to thank Thomas Keller and Laura Cunningham for conceiving these restaurants, giving me a job, and never looking over my shoulder. Forget all about finesse; you two *are* finesse.

To Carolyn Marino from HarperCollins and Paul Cirone from the Friedrich Agency, I would like to quote from *The Karate Kid*: Wax on, wax off.

Thanks to Mutti, Dad, Sam, my two pom-pom-carrying aunts, Barbara Damrosch and Anne Williams, and my cousin Jessica MacMurray Blaine, who not only writes beautifully about food, but can actually make things like salmon cornets.

I am awaiting karmic invoices from Sarah Norris, Suzie Guillette, Katie Akana, and Marci Delozier. Preferably in manuscript form.

At Sarah Lawrence, Vijay Seshadri, JoAnn Beard, Molly Haskell, and Rachel Cohen asked me the important questions.

For talking me down from high places, I'd like to thank Thea Stone and Kim Knittel.

Thank you to Susan Convery for being classmate, room-mate, boat mate, bike mate, soul mate, voice of unreason, and mistress of pronoia.

And finally, I would like to thank all those I have called "chef." The following is a list of the opening dining room staff of Per Se, a few latecomers and important chefs (the knife-carrying variety): Sonya Adams, Nate Begonia, Jonathan Benno, Kat Beto, Susan Blank, Yannick Broto, Virginia Bulli ner, Jose Carangui, Alex Castillo, Jorge Castillo, Natalie "Mama" Cox, Zion Curiel, Raj Dagstani, Michel Darmon, Peter Downey, Kate Edwards, Jeff Eichelberger, Peter Esmond, Matt Fuhrmann, Joe Gentry, Kerry Hamilton, James Hanley, Jimmy Hayes, Alisha Hidalgo, Tim Howard, E.J., Keith Kelly, Jill Kinney, Mahmud Lasker, James Lauer, Corey Lee, Chris L'Hommedieu, Eric Lilavois, Randy Logan, Leslie Lopez, Alisa Lozano, Lisa Mesiti, Rudy Mikula, Michael Minnillo, Kathryn Mirtsopoulos, Craig Muraszewski, Larry Nadeau, Emily New-man, David Norris, Paolo Novello, Arleene Oconitrillo, Asya Ollis, Kelly Pottle-Graham, "R-dog," Jose Reyes, Bill Rhodes, Paul Roberts, Anthony Rush, Rudy Santos, Veronica Santos, Joel Schott, Jonathan Schwartz, Joshua Schwartz, Lyndon Smith, Wayne Smith, Brendan Sodakoff, Linus Streckfus, Wil-son Thomas, Carolos Tomazos, Gregory Tomicich, Daniel Toral, Met Ture, Brian Van Flandern, Aracely Warner, and Tina Zekhtser.